PEACE! PEACE!

edited and compiled
by
FOY VALENTINE

WORD BOOKS WACO, TEXAS

WORD BOOKS • WACO, TEXAS
Library of Congress Catalog Card Number: 67-23975
Printed in U.S.A.

PREFACE

Peace is not only one of man's most elusive ideals but also one of his most enduring visions. The present volume has been prepared in an effort to help Christians of today's world to come to a better working knowledge of this great goal of peace and of the things that make for peace.

These chapters were first delivered as spoken messages at summer conferences on peace in Glorieta, New Mexico and Ridgecrest, North Carolina. Sponsored by the Christian Life Commission of the Southern Baptist Convention, these conferences sought to attract the most competent speakers available from across the nation. Most of the addresses retain, even in written form, the vigor and style of the spoken word. In editing, I have not tried to alter either the content or the style of these remarkably informative and expressive utterances. The various contributors might have used considerably different approaches if, from the beginning of their assignments, they had been writing their materials for a book. It is doubtful, however, that such an approach would have produced as vigorous and as useful a work as is here presented.

Special appreciation is hereby expressed to the contributors whose disciplined labors are responsible for any good that may come from this volume, to Mr. George Baskin who as WORD Books Director has given strong encouragement and excellent guidance to the early completion of this project, and to the Institute for International Order without whose generous support the conferences from which this book came could never have been conducted.

To the end that the Biblical prospect of peace on earth and good will among men may flourish in our time and to the end that Christians shall not be conformed to this warring world but rather be transformed to the ways of Him who is the Prince of Peace, this book is released in hope.

FOY VALENTINE

Table of Contents

1.

BIBLICAL INSIGHTS AND THE CONCEPT OF PEACE

CARLYLE MARNEY
Interpreter's House
Lake Junaluska, North Carolina
Former Pastor, Myers Park Baptist Church
Charlotte, North Carolina

I

Throughout this crucial period in race relations I have heard people asking "Why *this* issue? Why don't you preach on something harmless, like *peace*?"

I answer, "In a world like this, where our doorsteps are cluttered with specific persons in specific situations of specific conflict, to turn to a general term like *peace* is the way of evasion."

Yet it is good to see what can be said of the great hope which is peace, if we do not lose the local cruciality.

If we are going to think about Biblical concepts of peace, some ground rules are in order concerning what we mean by "peace" and what we understand about "power."

First: The peace of which the Bible speaks is not necessarily the kind of peace we imply in international relations. The Bible does not assume a kind of heavenly United Nations agreement.

Second: It would be a great mistake, on the other hand, to assume that the Bible is naive about power. Biblical writers knew a great deal about power and power structures and their inner workings. Consider the candor with which Joab, the back side of David's virtue, is presented within the power structure of ancient

Israel. Joab is there to make the king look good, and the Scripture makes no bones about this. Whenever the Bible talks about Assyria, or Babylon, or the Chaldeans, it exhibits a sophisticated knowledge of the historical contemporary power structures.

(It would be, though, equally as great a mistake to read Biblical materials as if Biblical people were as involved in power, intrigue, and cartels as contemporary man is. The ancients were not people of that same kind of power. Israel never argued from a vantage point similar to that of the United States, for example. She was never a world power. She was always an incident on the road to conquest for other major powers.)

Third: It would be a mistake to assume that the basic aim of the Bible is international peace. International peace is not a fundamental idea in the Bible; it is a derivative. God, and the people of God, are up to something to which that kind of peace is an incidental benefit.

Fourth: While one of our major contemporary desires is for peace, we must not assume that this same desire is at the center of the intent of Biblical writers. What the Bible calls *Mishala* (the desires of thine heart) are not necessarily our contemporary desires. We cannot really expect to find our American concerns, and desires, and interests corresponding to those of the ancient Hebrews. The Bible is an Oriental book. Our concerns and desires may not be Biblically desirable. Our legitimate concerns, as a nation or as the people of God, could conceivably be extra-Biblical, without being thereby irrelevant. Let us agree that we have to have a ground rule that lets us have the possibility of seeing that what we want may not be what the Bible is up to at all. But if that is so, it does not necessarily mean that what we want is irrelevant or unworthy or other than what the Biblical materials, if extended, would allow.

Fifth: We have to have a ground rule that lets us look for what we are talking about under some other word or term than "peace." The Bible may speak of what we are thinking about without using the word "peace."

Sixth: We must not assume that the word "peace" always means the same thing or that it always promises the same thing each place it is used in the Bible.

II

With those ground rules behind us, let us look at the terms with which the Bible stresses the general areas of conflict and contradiction.

First, the nouns—the substantives for peace:

Some of the terms for the people who are involved are: *the people; the nations; the kingdoms of the earth; sons of men; children of darkness; the hosts; the tongues; other tongues; strange tongues; the kings of the earth take council against the Lord and his anointed; the kingdoms of this world have become the sovereignty of our God and his Christ; all the kingdoms of the world.* Sometimes Scripture has in mind no particular political divisions, just whatever political divisions there happen to be. The Bible is not an intriguer. Whichever way the die has fallen, whichever way that is has broken open, whatever kingdoms there happen to be, are involved.

One would make a great mistake to try to find out what the Bible is talking about if he just checked out each appearance of the word "peace." Instead we must look to those places where *the will of Yahweh* is described. There we find the Biblical understanding of peace. Because, where there is complete conformity to *the will of the Lord* there is peace.

The way of the Lord—this is peace.

Or *the word of the law*—this is peace.

Other phrases carrying the connotation of the Biblical concept of peace are: *"Thus saith the Lord," "The one God," "The God who is one,"* or that favorite phrase in Jeremiah, *El Hay, "The Living."*

Wherever the *Lord's righteousness* is, there is peace.

Sometimes the Scripture speaks of the *Lord's Right* (what God has got coming to Him). There is peace.

Where the words *loving kindness* and *tender mercies* are used the Bible is talking about God's kind of peace.

The *day of the Lord,* or *the kingdom of God,* or *the kingdom of heaven,* or *the rule of Yahweh,* or *the arm of the Lord,* or *in that day*—all of these always refer to a day of peace.

There are other terms and places where peace is to be expected: *Zion; the Holy Hill; Mount Zion; the highway; the kingdom; the House of the Lord; the Temple of the Lord; the City of God; the sheep-fold; the mountain; the Holy mountain; the habitation; the fountain of the water of life.*

The people who are at peace with Yahweh are: *His flock; His people; His tribes; the kingdom; the nation; the church; the family; the children; sons and daughters.*

Let me reemphasize that you cannot simply find all the places the Bible uses the word "peace" and understand fully the Biblical concept of peace. Consider, for example, the relevant verbs: *rage; defile; make war; destroy; invade; rule; overthrow; tread softly; send the sword; violence; graze; rest; assemble; find pasture; send; give; rejoice; lie down; give thanks; make war no more; move in and out.* (Peace is something one *does* in the Bible, frequently, rather than a frictionless state of passivity.)

Then there are certain significant adjectives and adverbs: *haughty; proud; eyes standing out with fatness; mincing walk; wheeled instruments of war.*

Sometimes the things that make for un-peace are *armed* and sometimes they are *horsed.*

(There are perhaps a hundred words that could be added in each of these sections.)

III

Let us next look at six fundamental Biblical concepts that are related to peace.

1. The first one is *theodicy.* One aim of Scripture is to reconcile the existence of evil in the world with the goodness and justice of God. From the point of view of the writers of Scripture, it was

to make our God look good to the heathen. This was a tremendous problem during the captivity. "Where is now your God?"

The Psalms, more than any of the Biblical writings, are literally packed with this. Scan the Psalms and see how many of them aim to justify God. (Biblical writers hammered out their affirmations of theodicy on the anvil of experience. Jeremiah, for example, discovered that prayer is as much curse as it is blessing. Sometimes Jeremiah's prayers are delivered with a clenched fist. He knows God is great enough to understand his anger. He knows that a man who knows God doesn't have to "pussy-foot" with the Almighty. He can say what lies in his innards.) And this is what the Bible is up to when it sets out to make God look good. In Psalm 114, "The mountains skipped like rams" when God led us out. In Psalm 115, in the face of all our evidence, why should the nations even have to ask what our God is like? Isn't it perfectly obvious? In Psalm 118, or 135, or 139, or 145, or 147, or 148, or 149, or 150, this theodicy is all over the place. How eager these believers in the Eternal are for God to be acceptable to the heathen on the basis of His justice.

The classic theodicy and the most beautiful Psalm in the book is 126. This is a free translation. "When the Lord returned us to Zion, when the Lord turned us loose from Babylon, when we started out on the road to return us to Zion, we were like dreamers. Our mouths spilled over laughter. Our laughter was too big for our mouths. And our tongues were flopping with their singing. Our tongues wouldn't be still. Our tongues were loose at both ends. For the *goyim* were saying, 'Their Lord has done big things.'" This is the aim of Scripture. This is why we are glad: not just that we have been turned loose after a seventy-year captivity; not alone that this agony is over; but that *now God has come out in the open and has done this!* The heathen can only say HOW GREAT YOUR GOD! See? This is what filled the heart of these people. Our God looks good to the heathen. "This is why we are glad, therefore," they said, "sowing tears, reaping joy: go forth crying, but carrying your seed for sowing; come again with joy, bringing your sheaves with you." That's the way it is. This is the world of peace.

I have a neighbor on Hyder Mountain, a Russian Jew, graduate of the University of London in Economics, the Warsaw School of Forestry, chief liaison for the British armies during the war in the Mediterranean, who uses about fourteen languages. He is convinced that God is *one* and that this *oneness* permeates the earth and that this is the essence of Judaism; and, that Judaism, when it is full grown, transcends all our little categories, so *He* belongs to all the nations. He says the one word he sees acted out all over the world among Jews is *"pen yomru ha goyim,"* "What will the Gentiles say? We Jews are always reacting to our neighbors. What will the Gentiles say?" Move this into Biblical language, emphasize it, and this is the reason that they desire their God to look good. They want their God to look good, to make God's justice apparent to the nations, because even then they are under the pressure of being a different people. This is a Biblical feeling. Now, when God's actions are perceived, even by the Gentiles, as good, there will be peace.

2. Another basic concept is the rule of Yahweh. This is a general term for all kinds of kingdom words. *The kingdom of God, God's power over the nations,* the essential triumph of *the oneness, the rule of Yahweh,* is constantly being referred to in the Bible. *The earth shall be full* or *the Gentiles shall come* or whether you follow the chiliastic expectancy of the millenialist, or the Davidic kingdom, *peace* would come under any of these extremes. The notion was that the rule of Yahweh, or the Kingdom of God, would be manifest among the nations. Meanwhile, in the Old Testament, God already has this power. When Assyria has done what Assyria is going to do God will put His hook in her nose, His bridle in her teeth, and ride her back to the East whence she came. In the meantime, He has this power over the Chaldeans, the Babylonians, and the Egyptians. Whatever happens serves the will of God in the Old Testament.

But the triumph of the oneness is another thing. Victor Frankl's narrative of his years in the concentration camps tells that on the day he was arrested an old jacket that he had worn, stuffed with the sheets of a manuscript, was snatched from him. Given a substitute jacket to wear, he despaired of his book, but weeks later, fumbling around in the lining of the jacket, he found a flyleaf of a Hebrew prayer book, bearing the great prayer, "Hear, O Israel: The Lord our God is one Lord; And thou shalt love the Lord thy God with all thine heart . . ." This is the thing around which peace will always rest as it comes. (There are 180 verses in John's Gospel alone in the context of which Jesus is obsessed to know and to do the will of the Father. He is absolutely carried off with the idea, "I am come down from heaven not to do my own will, but the will of him who sent me.") Frankl said he took the discovery of that page to mean that he was supposed to *live* that book he had been trying to *write*, and who can say that he didn't? This is the rule of Yahweh.

3. The third great concept that we have to work with is the concept of the covenant and the covenant people. Now, covenant and law are much a part of what the prophets thought and taught. They assumed the place of covenant in the life of Israel. But they also preached that covenant had been perverted and misunderstood, especially in the mouths of those they called derisively *nabi-Yahweh*. The man-made "prophets of the Lord" ruined it. Yet, the notion of covenant was there. It was never in any systematized theology that rested on Exodus, or the Davidic throne, or the temple; but Jeremiah says (Jeremiah 3:16) that there would come a time when the ark would be no more remembered, or visited, or recovered, or made, or even thought about; the ark of the covenant would disappear as a symbol. I suppose he means a temple or a tent of meeting would come, but then the tent meeting would be the ground; and then a people of Yahweh, of covenant, of righteousness in which God gets what is coming to him, would be the basis for any kind of peace.

4. The fourth major concept with which we have to work is the Messianic hope. Not Messiah, yet; but the hope of Messiah.

The Lord's anointed, whether he was Cyrus, or some new ruler with aspirations like Theudas, who arose in the first Christian century, was still the Lord's anointed; and every notch on this pole is filled. There is a cacophony of expectant voices here. Dom Gregory Dix claims that if Jesus had had any political aspiration at all, what happened six centuries later could have happened as well in the first century A.D. Behind a wall of Semitic nationalism there arose more fervor than Mormonism or Jehovah's Witnesses raised in this country. That could have happened in the first century as easily as it happened in the sixth century. If Christ had not been absolutely compelled by his obsession with the spiritual rule of Yahweh, he could, with the slightest bit of political ambition, have been the head of a vast new political region and a religion supported by Semitic tribes in the millions that could have swallowed the Roman Empire. But always this expectancy of Messiah's millennium was as nearly national as Jewishness ever became, and it was always supernatural. They had no clear political theory for this world of peace, but one thing sure, it was a theocracy. The only kind of government they thought about was a theocracy.

5. A fifth basic concept is the ethic of obedience. There are two aspects of faith, the active voice and the passive voice. Faith in the active voice is the life of obedience. It is the arena within which one does what he does because he has been given. There is no such thing as peace apart from obedience.

6. The last concept is the new human race, or the responsibility of the image. Those who are made in the image of God have a responsibility. We have been perfectly willing for God to have peace, for the world to have peace, for all the tribes of Africa to have peace, for our neighbors to have peace, if this can be achieved without personal involvement on our part. The classic example of this is the old fellow who says, "I'm perfectly willing for everybody to get it just like I got it." The responsibility of the image, the new human race where dwelleth righteousness, is a concept to which we must return.

IV

Christianity was not the product of the class struggle. At no point was the new religion directly concerned with the social upheavals of the ancient world. It was involved with something else. There was no formulating of the social question. The great problem in Christianity in its earliest stages was purely religious. There was no attempt to improve the whole world or to heal everybody. The primitive Christian communities had very little to do with the most important socio-historical events of the imperial world. The Christian church had nothing to do with the disappearance of the peasant classes, or with the reduction in the number of slaves, or with the development of slavery to serfdom. The Christian church had nothing to do with the transfer of capital to the owners of large estates, or the creation of the great middle class, or the withdrawal of power from the coast towns to the interior towns, or the changes of civil and military life, or the return to rural life.

Christianity as a religion is not a social phenomenon. It did not offer a transforming social ideal, like equality. Christian faith has never genuinely received equality, I think. It offers no freedom, nor painlessness, nor satisfaction which comes by divine effort in the absence of human accomplishment. If it had offered this it would have relieved us of all responsibility. But the Christian faith never set out to say, "You wait; God will do it." Instead, the Christian ideal means the renunciation of dependence upon all political and economic forms. This is why there can be a church underground. The Christian faith has never been dependent upon a political ideology for its existence. All political and economic values are to be seen as simple tools, and there is a turning toward the religious treasure of peace of heart, love of humanity, fellowship with God. These are the big things. There are general social problems that belong to the world and will perish with the world. The New Testament doesn't care about the state at all, as such. Jewish nationalism is ignored entirely, and the communism that is in the New Testament is a communism of *consumers,* not producers, and there is a difference. They still made what they made by private enterprise, if anyone wants to make a point of it. It only became a communism when they began to consume what they made. It was, if anything, a communism of love.

Yet, the whole thing rested on monotheism, which was belief in the one God, the basis for independence of personality and belief in a new universal humanity—a new human race. This is an inescapable category of all Biblical thought. Whatever peace we get is the peace that derives from a new human race. There was a spirit of freedom and a spiritual fellowship in which tyranny, law, war, and force were unknown. Beginning with Paulinism, a new and rich ethos was working up in Biblical thought. But the key is that nowhere in the New Testament or the Old Testament is there the expectancy that God would do something that we were not able to do.

V

Now with that key, let us look back at what this says in the way of a baptized and Biblical humanism. "For unto us a child is born, unto us a son is given: and the government shall be upon his shoulder: and his name shall be called Wonderful, Counselor, The mighty God, The everlasting Father, The Prince of Peace" (Isaiah 9:6). And this is the point, it is *unto us* that the child is born; no mistake. It is *unto us* that the son is given and his name shall *by us* be called Wonderful, Counselor, Mighty God, Everlasting Father, Prince of Peace. In no truly effective way does Christ the Lord have these names until they are given to him by us. Something eternal is in our hands. This eternal theme is in our hands—it is *unto us.* It is not novelty. This humanism is in essence a new agency, a new freedom, a new responsibility. God has put His future, Himself, in our hands. A child is born *unto us.* A son is born *unto us.* And at our house we wouldn't know what to do with one. What would we do with a baby? And this is the history of Christendom!

We are really not accustomed to being so responsible for our gifts. What does it matter what God calls the Son unless we call Him the same thing? This Eternal gets His character and His name from us. What good to say in our prayers Wonderful, Counselor, Almighty God, Everlasting Father, Prince of Peace, what good unless He is this to us? And He is this by us, for in our hands He receives His character and His name. Where can we go to be rid of this? The whole church is still in a kind of post partum shock. The Biblical message makes us agonizingly responsible for God's having His way in His world. How can we evade this unto us-ness? How can we protect ourselves from the claims of this Holy child?

We can become reformed theologians; this will do it. We can say that God has done it. Hallelujah! Yahweh is my God! He has done it. He has given it. All we have to do is receive. We can, as the Baptists of my boyhood were in danger of doing, drop the whole beautiful ethic of obedience out of Holy Scripture and forget to preach that there are things that you have to do. We can become reformed theologians and say that God has done it.

Or there is an amazingly similar thing: we can join in a kind of federal morality in which everything is settled for us at headquarters—whether the headquarters be your denominational headquarters or Washington, D. C. We can become victims of the kind of federalized morality in which everything is cut at headquarters and all you have to do for yourself is sew it up and wear it—what is good, what is bad, what is right, what is wrong.

Or we can evade our responsibility by adopting a confederate culture. Now by a confederate culture, I don't mean the old Southern Confederacy. I mean a confederation of all our local values where Christ is baptized and initiated into the church with our color, our accent, our theology, our tongue, our thoughts, our loyalties, and our values. We can escape Christ by making Him just like us. Make Him just like us and He won't bother us. This we have done. God knows we have done this.

And, if all then fail, we can escape Him by falling off into what I would call an objective neurosis. By this, humanity has always evaded its great demands. We can hide our competency with our illness. Paul Tournier talks about it. He says he has patients who would hand over their insides to anybody, any magician who would promise to heal them. This is the way we evade. Dostoevsky talks about the ill-fated creature who runs every time freedom comes by. Now when we do this to Him, in our hands He becomes a thing, an "it," a tool. Christ is an escape, or a substitute, or a scapegoat, or a magician, or an excuser, or an alibi. We keep looking outside ourselves for responsibility and decision. We can't, with integrity, evade our responsibility. Jesus Christ gets His face in today's world from those who name Him. What use is it for God to call Him "Son" if we name Him "visionary fool"? What use is it for God and history to call Him its center if we make Him useless? What use is it for the church to call Him Lord for 2,000 years, if we persist in making Him mere legend? Can we not make His work of no effect for us? This is not to defeat the great God. It is simply suicide for us. It is not regicide—we don't kill off God. We just kill off ourselves, and here is the point; it is *unto us* that a Child is born, *unto us* that a Son is given and His name shall *by us* be called Prince of Peace. Our first duty is to name Him.

Peace does not wait on God. It waits on us. Paul says the whole creation waits on the sons of God to grow up and act like it. God waits on us, and this is incredible and frightening. It is, however, the only basic Biblical concept of peace that I can see. What if God loves us so much that He lets us beat ourselves to death, rather than letting us be less than people? Everything that the Bible demands makes men, men of responsibility and decision and obedience and action. Paul says the whole creation stands on its tiptoes to see the wonderful sight of the sons of God as they come into their own. But the sons of God who come into their own are grown men with responsible decisions and action behind them. Peace is in our hands, Biblically.

Peace, Biblical peace, Christian peace, has never been national. Peace has never been an external condition. It is not just an act or deed. It is not even a goal. Biblical peace is not an achievement. It is internal, rather than external. It is an attitude which results in peaceful acts. It is a result, not a goal. It is an inheritance, not an achievement. It is a spiritual operation, not a condition. It is a way of life, not a contracted agreement.

In times of drought, primitive people used to send their magicians up in trees with buckets of water. Their function was to pray, wildly and long, while between cries they tipped their buckets to spill a little water down to prime the pumps of heaven and make it rain. But rain doesn't come that way. And neither does peace. Our magicians have met from Dumbarton Oaks to Paris, from San Francisco and London to Potsdam, and the buckets have been thoroughly tipped. Indeed, they are well nigh empty, but peace doesn't come this way and neither does rain. Rain comes up from the earth in droplets, drawn by the sun, before they descend to earth as rain, and so does peace. The waters of peace come up like the dew from the ground where even the grains of sand are individual. Peace is a matter for persons. It has always been a matter for persons. It can become a matter for nations only as it becomes a climate of reality between persons. How can there be peace between nations when there is no peace in the state? And how can there be peace in Carolina before there is peace in Mecklenburg County? How can there be peace in Mecklenburg County until there is peace in Charlotte? How can there be peace in Charlotte until there is peace in Myers Park? How can there be peace in Myers Park until there is peace in me? How can there be peace in me until I have been related to the Source of peace?

Peace, we said, has never been external. Most external conditions of international peace have been conditions of either domination or exhaustion. In spite of Pax Romana and Pax Brittanica, peace is inside or it simply is not. No society can survive the chaos produced when its members treat each other as groups treat other groups today. The trick is to learn to treat other groups as we must treat each other. But it begins within. A man would not survive five minutes in some sections of our society if he acted toward individuals as some of us have acted toward other denominations, and other races, and other nations. And who could survive if he treated his next door neighbor as he was taught to behave towards Germans and Japanese? What we call holy cannot survive another fifty years of our treating each other as nations like we have treated each other as persons. Peace has to come from an inner source. It is internal, not external.

Therefore, peace is an attitude before it is an act. One day a man approached his emperor crying, "*Ave Emperator*"; that was an act of peace and a sign of peace. But the inner attitude was not peace and the next act was a knife in the back of Julius Caesar. The act of peace for Japan was to keep her emissaries dealing with the old Tennessean, Cordell Hull, in Washington. But there was no peace in spite of acts of peace. Attitude had already determined Pearl Harbor.

Peace, more than this, is a resultant inheritance, not an achieved goal. According to the Biblical language, it is a spiritual operation. Peace has never been a matter of getting all the Methodists to unite with all the Baptists. Even before the Nicene Council in 325 A.D., Christianity had ninety different frames, each of which was heresy to the remaining majority and each of which had some grasp of Messiah at its heart. Peace is a spiritual operation, not a condition of this kind of unity. It's an act of faith, says the Chinaman, Lin Yutang, but it so happens that we are a generation almost without faith; and without faith who can be saved?

Peace is not something that I agree to keep. It's a way of life as the result of something that I have been given; it is the spiritual operation of faith, not a condition of state. It is, therefore, neither national, nor external, nor act, nor achievement, nor condition. Peace is first individual, internal, a corporate attitude, an inheritance, a lived way. It is something that happens to you as the result of being in touch with its Source. Sometimes I think it can't come at all until you're in your late forties. But it is so wonderful a thing that it is understandable that those who do not have it should look for it. And those who will not receive it should be forced to go without it. For Christianity, according to the teachings of Jesus, has never promised external conditions of peace except as the peace that comes from the people of God, up. The world order has never been such that it could be called Christian. The powers that be have never belonged to Him. Always He has worked through them, in spite of them, on the individual grains of sand.

Christianity is not responsible for producing world peace in the New Testament. For Christianity is war. God versus mammon. Alter versus ego. I against me. Good against evil. The man who could be who opposes the man I am. Sometimes it is war against stupidity. But it is the war that produces peace, the only way war can ever produce peace, by surrender.

The claims of our Lord set a man against himself, I discover. They split him down the middle. They make him schizoid. Once he faces up to the claims of Christ he is divided, he is at war, until surrender. He can never be justified by what he does: his new gadgets, his nursery rhyme creeds, his one-eyed philosophies, his mud-pie civilization, his kindergarten councils. He can be justified only in himself, and his justification begins only when he is a man of peace, and his peace comes only when he surrenders to the Source of peace against which he fights.

Harnack said forty years ago that Jesus Christ searches for the point in every man where he may lay hold and begin leading him into the Kingdom of God. He lays hold of him at the point of his greatest need: dominion of demons, fear of death, life, error, night, sin, perversion, emptiness. Beginning with his lack of peace, beginning where he is, He leads him into the available peace, the kind of peace that I used to hear Peter Marshall call "a garrison from within to defend us."

This peace is in the Advent, "Peace among men of good will."

It is in the teaching, "Blessed are the makers of peace" (happy are those who have begun to reproduce the peace that garrisons). There are thirty-one forms of the word in the Scriptures. I have counted 393 verses where the word "peace" is central. It was awfully important to Christ. It is in His death. "Peace I leave with you, my peace I give unto you: not as the world giveth, give I unto you" (John 14:27). But it was in accord with the mind of Jesus, I think, and at the same time a fact of history, that gospel peace should come only in connection with a believing surrender to the person of Christ. The Father has promised His peace to such sons. But a man has to surrender to get his wings. This is the galling part. A man has to give in, as simply as Simeon did the day he met the parents of Jesus and took the child in his arms. Surrendering to whatever he got, mostly the expectancy that had inhabited him, I suppose, he sang the *Nunc dimittis,* that immortal first Christian hymn, "Lord, now lettest thou thy servant depart in peace, according to thy word, for mine eyes have seen thy salvation" (Luke 2:29-30).

In the Gospel we are impressed not that Jesus loved, not that Jesus was humble, not that Jesus was merciful. We are impressed that *he loved the Father like nothing else.* One hundred and eighty verses in John's Gospel alone are in the context of this obsession, this love of the Father and His will. He loved the Father, radically, and Him he radically obeyed. We, in the Gospel, are called not to love our neighbors as our God; we are to love our neighbors as we love ourselves. *We are to love God as we love nothing else.* Mercy, justice, compassion, and humility are all to proceed from the love of the Father. The unchanging Christian concept is that in Jesus Christ men come to know their Father, whose love and mercy they reflect. Everything else changes. This is radical monotheism, as Dr. Richard Niebuhr called it. This is radical love. This is a love that derives its strength to love from the love which is its source. This is the unchanging love which can move us into the world of peace.

Faith is still paradoxical; and still dynamic. Faith can have peace and cannot have peace. In this agony every day you have to be born again. Old answers, in the present urgency, become new, and this is what Soren Kierkegaard calls "believer's realism." The fact that you call yourself a believer bears witness to the fact that you are on a journey. What you look for is not here, which is precisely the reason you believe it. If it were here you wouldn't have to believe it. Faith signifies the blessed unrest which urges the believer with, "No rest here." As in Exodus, moving toward some kind of peace, God speaks, but does not bellow at us.

Where then is the peace? The peace comes in seeing all parts in the light of the whole. This is the universal sacrament from within which one can live in the peace of a defended fortress. Here we could discover our local community as an instrument being sharpened in God's hands to *make* social and personal righteousness.

"The government shall be upon his shoulders." "At the name of Jesus every knee shall bow." "Sit thou on my right hand until I make the earth thy footstool." "The earth shall be full of the knowledge of the Lord as waters cover the sea." Why doesn't God give us peace? What if He has done it already and the dodging church is His most serious problem? Christianity needs a new infusion of passionate obedience, for as it is, we just keep burying ourselves. George Bernard Shaw once said that we might as well go out into the garden and dig until it is time to dig our graves unless we can change.

For what have you truly lived? This is your God. Here are the true breaks with tradition and habit and conformity. These are not larger problems than we have already handled. The government is on His shoulders. But we are His means of performance. This requires something that we have hardly faced at all. But it is our only hope for peace, that we can become obediently responsible.

2.

THE BIBLE SPEAKS ON WAR AND PEACE

JIMMY R. ALLEN
Secretary of the Christian Life Commission
Baptist General Convention of Texas
Dallas, Texas

Herman Kahn, the noted weapons analyst, has produced a book about the strategy of nuclear warfare entitled *Thinking About the Unthinkable* (New York: Horizon Press, 1962).

To think about the unthinkable is exactly what we are being called upon to do in a world under the shadow of a nuclear question mark. For some, the problem is "unthinkable" because of the limitations of our minds in comprehending a situation in which all of civilization could be annihilated. The new vocabulary of the nuclear age now includes the word "megacorpses," meaning "a million dead." This is unthinkable to many of us.

For many of us the problem is unthinkable because of its vast complexity and intricate technology. We can no longer afford to occupy our energies with superficial generalizations. The problem demands a great deal more factual knowledge than is available for most of us. Even when that knowledge is available, it is still a difficult and demanding task to think it through. Therefore, the problem is "unthinkable" and we retreat into the busy world of ordinary details hoping that if we keep looking the other way, the problem will disappear.

For most of us the problem has become "unthinkable" because

of the sense of helplessness bordering on despair which has beset us. What could one man do even if he does think about the unthinkable? There seems to be no practical possibility of implementing our conclusions in the collective behavior of mankind. It becomes much easier to leave this to the leaders and criticize them at every opportunity!

The task to which we now set ourselves is to think through the concept of peace. We do so with the conviction that this is a goal toward which Christians should be striving. The immediate task is to consider Biblical insights in the concept of peace.

It may seem the height of irrelevance to discuss what the Bible says about war and peace in a world in which the live options being discussed center on whether nuclear war should be counterforce or countercity; the possibilities of limited strategic city reprisal; the exchange of cities in nuclear destruction; and controlled or unlimited countercity retaliation. All of this is far removed from Galilean villages of another era in which professional armies met on the bloody battlefields of the plains of Megiddo to decide the supremacy of minor kings in small countries.

For many persons, peace simply does not seem to be a live option, and all the old concepts of this discussion sound strangely hollow in the harsh light of hydronuclear facts. Yet for those of us who believe that the Bible is the inspired Word of God, the principles of God must be perceived so that they can be applied in the midst of the complexities of our kind of world.

Let us examine what the Bible says. We shall discover that the Bible is being used and misused in dealing with the problems of war and peace, that the Biblical ideal is peace, and that believers should search for a Christian posture in a warring world.

I. THE USE OF THE BIBLE IN DEALING WITH THE PROBLEM OF WAR AND PEACE

There are few questions concerning which the Bible has been "used" as much as those centering in the problem of war and peace. Men have made pretzels out of the passages of God's

Word, twisting them to fit the need of the moment both for and against warfare. Christian history repeats over and over the pathetic picture of prophets of God using the pulpit to justify their national policies as the cause of righteousness. The picture is especially tragic when the two nations are church-oriented so that the "prophets" on each side are invoking the curse of the same God upon their enemy. On the other hand, the pacifists of a few decades ago, basing their optimism on a superficial view of the evil inherent in mankind, used the Scriptures to prove that the *summum bonum* of all humanity is nonviolence. They were seized with the fantasy that violent conflict was going to be sloughed off forever. Their misuse of the Bible was just as real as that of the proponents of the "just" war.

Indeed, the reaction against such misuse of the Bible has produced a paralysis in the churches concerning this whole problem. Dr. Paul Peachy points this out in his report of a colloquy called by the Church Peace Mission when he says, "The security of today's theology of tragedy is based in no small measure on the determination of theologians not be 'taken in' again."[1]

1. Absence of Systematic Treatment of War and Peace

A factor in the misuse of the Bible is that there is no systematic treatment of the problem of war and peace in the Bible. Like many other social issues, the problem of war is treated only incidentally and by implication. One reason is that Christians in the New Testament era were not forced to face the question of participation in warfare. C. J. Cadoux points out that not only were Jews and slaves exempt from service in the Roman legions, but also that the Roman government seldom found it necessary to resort to conscription to fill the ranks of its armies.[2] The Roman army was also the police power of that day so that basic law and order depended upon this form of armed might. To condemn

---

[1]Paul Peachy, "Peacemaking: a Church Calling," *Christian Century*, Vol. LXXX, No. 31 (July 31, 1963), p. 953.

[2]C. J. Cadoux, *Early Christian Attitudes Toward War* (London: Headley Bros. Publishers, Ltd., 1919), p. 41.

one would mean to condemn the other. Christians, then, lived in a world of military might without having to face the question of personal relationship to this problem.

Whether this is the reason for it or not, the absence of a clear word in a systematic fashion about Christian participation in war or the method for attaining peace has created a climate in which every shade of opinion has flourished.

2. The Use of the Bible to Justify War

It is common for Christians to search the Scriptures for justification for participation in war. It is important to examine these arguments.

(1) *Old Testament Wars Commanded by God*

One of the most commonly used Scriptural arguments for war is that God commanded Israel to wage wars of extermination (Joshua 8:1-2, 10:40, I Samuel 15:3). Some contend that if there were something basically evil about war God would not have commanded Israel to participate in it.

It must be conceded that these commands of God do constitute a problem of major proportions to the interpreter who believes both in the *agape* nature of God and the validity of Scriptural account. Some have rejected the Old Testament picture of God because of this problem. In the early days of church history, the Manichaeans "affirmed that they represented Jehovah in such a strange character that the God of the Old Testament could not be the loving and redeeming God of the New Testament."[3] In more modern times the pacifist Kirby Page concurs with this judgment saying, "The God of Jesus differs fundamentally from the Jehovah presented in many sections of the Old Testament where Yahweh is frequently pictured as authorizing pillage and slaughter."[4]

Others feel that Israel was mistaken in their interpretation of what God told them to do. William H. P. Faunce says, "Israel did

[3]W. S. Bruce, *The Ethics of the Old Testament* (New York: Scribner, 1928), p. 283.

[4]Kirby Page, *Jesus or Christianity* (Garden City, New York: Doubleday, Doran and Co., Inc., 1929), p. 16.

receive command to oppose the foulness of surrounding idolatries and cleave unto its own real God, and the only way of doing this appeared to be the method then adopted by every human tribe—the method of ruthless extermination."[5]

W. S. Bruce searches for a moral argument which would justify the extermination of the Amalekites and points out the exceedingly great patience of God in giving space for repentance from the day of Abraham to the day of Joshua.[6]

None of these positions is fully satisfactory. Answers to this moral question which center in a rejection of the accuracy of the inspired record, or presume that Israel misunderstood God's intention, or search for a thread of moral justification in the light of God's complete revelation of himself all miss the mark. But so does the argument that modern nuclear destruction can be justified on the basis of the wars of Israel. If we are going to return to the concept of morality in these early stages of God's self-revelation, many kinds of morally bizarre behavior could be justified. It certainly should be obvious to us that the New Testament is not to be interpreted in the light of the Old, but the Old in the light of the New.

The key to understanding this question of Old Testament wars lies in an understanding of progressive revelation. God had to meet men on the level of comprehension which they had. He was purposing to work through one nation to build a concept of himself so that he could eventually complete his revelation in the sending of his Son. In order to do this, it became necessary to secure a separation of this nation from the idolatrous nations around them. An unusual act of moral surgery had to be performed for the preservation of God's revelation in the life of this chosen nation. Bruce is right when he says, "Either the Canaanites were to be spared to contaminate Israel with their abominations until the latter nation became wholly unfit to be

---

[5]William H. P. Faunce, *Religion and War* (New York: Abingdon Press, 1918), p. 16.

[6]Bruce, *op. cit.*, p. 287.

the instrument of revelation, or they must be swept off the face of the earth. To spare them would have been to imperil the hope of the world's salvation."[7]

There is absolutely no parallel between the military position of ancient Israel and that of modern nations. The enemies whom Israel fought were God's enemies and this fact saved them from the brutalizing effects of participating in this slaughter. Rutenber says, "It must be carefully underscored that the teaching of the Old Testament is that the enemies against whom the Hebrews fight are God's enemies, not their own . . . There is nothing in the Old Testament to teach the Hebrews that they have the right . . . to fight their own enemies."[8] For any modern nation to use this Scriptural teaching for justification of the unleashing of modern warfare is to assume an omniscience and a righteousness as the one instrument of God in the world. Such an assumption is indefensible.

(2) *The Prediction of Wars and Rumors of Wars*

When describing the coming judgment, Jesus predicted that there would be wars and rumors of wars to the end of the age (Matthew 24:6-7). Some have used this prediction as justification for warfare. However, Jesus was simply making a statement of fact. This does not imply divine sanction for the situation. There were other occasions when he spoke of persecutions and sufferings in the future. This did not imply his approval of the situation. A similar argument centers in the failure to condemn the military in the New Testament. Jesus commends the faith of a Roman centurion without condemning his profession (Matthew 8:5). John the Baptist had excellent occasion to pronounce opposition to war when the soldiers asked what they should do to be right with God. He simply answered that they were to do violence to no man, accuse no man falsely, and be content with their wages (Luke 3:14).

Herschberger claims that John the Baptist did demand a sever-

---

[7]Bruce, *op. cit.*, p. 288.

[8]C. G. Rutenber, *The Dagger and the Cross* (New York: Fellowship Publications, 1950), p. 72.

ance from the military life. He says, "When he told the soldiers to 'do violence to no man' he would seem to have made it impossible for them to continue as soldiers. Violence and the military profession definitely belong together."[9] Most scholars, however, disagree with Herschberger's interpretation at this point.

To use this argument from silence either as a justification or as a condemnation of war is to assume a dangerous position. The New Testament is silent about too many things for this line of reasoning to be utilized. Jesus did not condemn a woman taken in the act of adultery, but this does not mean that he approved prostitution. Slavery is not condemned in the Bible but the principles revealed in the New Testament were the moving force in its abolition.

(3) *The Command to Sell Cloaks to Buy a Sword*

One of the frequently used justifications for war in the New Testament is the passage which depicts Jesus on the night of his betrayal commanding the disciples, "He that hath no sword, let him sell his garment and buy one" (Luke 22:35-38). The disciples state that they have two swords in their possession. He then says either, "It is enough" or, "Enough of this." It is argued that the passage provides for prudential self-defense and justifies defensive warfare.

The pacifist has a dilemma in interpreting this passage. The elasticity of Scriptural interpretation is seldom stretched to such fantastic proportions as in the handling of this passage. There are as many interpretations as there are interpreters.

Scott-Craig says that this is an ironic reference to the similarity between the appearance of this group and that of the robber bands which roamed Palestine. He sees Christ as thinking in pictures in referring to the bags, scripts, and swords. Later Jesus questions the soldiers as to the reason for their coming with weapons to take him. "Do we look like robbers?"[10]

---

[9]Guy F. Herschberger, *War, Peace, and Nonresistance* (Scottdale, Penn: The Herald Press, 1946), p. 353.

[10]T. S. K. Scott-Craig, *Christian Attitude to War and Peace* (New York: Charles Scribner's Sons, 1938), p. 42.

Herschberger sees this as another reference to the fact that the disciples are not grasping the spiritual nature of the Kingdom. He believes Christ is complaining about the weakness of their vision. He says, "This may have been his way of telling Peter that he knew all about his hidden sword . . . Perhaps the meaning was like this, 'If you have no more faith than this, what more can I say?' At any rate, from Jesus' life and teaching, it is impossible to believe that he approved the carrying of swords."[11]

John Graham, the Quaker, sees the passage as the product of a discouraged Christ overtaken by the feeling of defeat as he came under the shadow of the cross. In his weariness and knowledge of the ordeal to come, the despair of the hour which is at hand shines through. Graham says, "They were to take money and provision as the worldly wise do, for it was all over with him."[12] When the moment of the trial comes, Jesus is revived in his spirit and condemns the use of the sword.

C. G. Rutenber, who believes in non-violent resistance, sees in this passage no grounds for arming for self-defense. He argues, "(1) When Peter used his sword in the garden, Jesus rebuked him. (2) Jesus told Pilate that his Kingdom was not of this world else would his servants fight. (3) If Christ meant the saying literally, he cruelly underestimated the opposition. (4) If Jesus seriously entertained the idea of armed resistance here, it was in direct conflict with the whole pattern of his teachings and life. In a living, picturesque metaphor, Jesus was warning his disciples of the seriousness of the hour."[13]

Regardless of how one interprets the statement of Jesus about the swords, the use of the passage to justify the annihilation of the guilty and the innocent in modern warfare is completely out of order. Even if it were a justification of prudential self-defense, it would not be a justification of both resisting an aggressor and also rushing out to destroy the aggressor's family and friends.

---

[11]Herschberger, *op. cit.*, p. 355.

[12]John W. Graham, *War From a Quaker Point of View* (London: Headley Bros., n. d.), p. 18.

[13]Rutenber, *op. cit.*, p. 81.

Reinhold Niebuhr is not a pacifist. He contends, however, that to base one's interpretation of participation in war on whether Jesus said, "Enough of this" or "It is enough" is too precarious a foundation for such an important question.[14]

(4) *The Command to Respect the State*

From the days of Constantine, Christians have sought to justify war on the grounds of the commands of the Bible to respect and give allegiance to the state. Jesus says that men are to render unto Caesar the things that are Caesar's and unto God what is God's (Matthew 22:21). Paul reminds men that the powers that be are ordained of God (Romans 13). The reasoning follows that since the citizen enjoys the privilege of government and gives his allegiance to government, he owes to the state his obedience. Therefore, in warfare he becomes the instrument of the state. If he kills in battle, it is not he but the state that does it.

Such arguments beg the question. "They solve the question before they grapple with it. The question is, 'Is it unchristian to go to war?' If it is, then the state must be resisted for we must obey God rather than man."[15] The Bible leaves no room for doubt the highest allegiance is to God.

While there are a number of other arguments used in which the Bible is misused to justify war, examination reveals that each must be twisted out of context to make it relate to the problem of war. The problem must be approached not from a "proof-text" method but from the spirit of the New Testament. Reinhold Niebuhr is correct when he says that "we are very foolish if we try to reduce the ethic [of the New Testament] so that it will cover and justify our prudential and relative standards and strategies."[16]

3. *The Use of the Bible to Condemn War*

The pacifist is no less guilty of reading into each passage a

[14]Reinhold Niebuhr, *Christianity and Power Politics* (New York: Charles Scribner's Sons, 1940), p. 14.

[15]Rutenber, *op. cit.*, p. 81.

[16]Niebuhr, *op. cit.*, p. 9.

condemnation of war and using the Bible for justifying his position. While the spirit of the New Testament does condemn war, the proof texts used are often erroneous. Let us examine some of these.

(1) *Jesus' Refusal to Be Crowned an Earthly King*

In the Temptation experience (Matthew 4:8-10), Jesus was offered the kingdoms of the world if he would bow before Satan. The pacifist often interprets this rejection by Jesus to be a rejection of the method necessary for attaining the kingdoms of the world. T. W. Manson says that Jesus discerned in this temptation "a capitulation to methods and aims—militarism, hatred, revolt against Rome."[17] Cadoux says that it is "difficult to imagine any other ground" for the refusal of Jesus to fall before this temptation than "the conviction that there was something immoral, something contrary to the will of God, in the use of the only means by which world rule could then be obtained, namely the waging of a successful war."[18]

Jesus refused the leadership of the masses as an earthly king at other times. After the feeding of the five thousand, he rejected their demand that he become their king (John 6:15). He chose at the triumphal entry to ride a donkey instead of a white charger (John 11:12-14). The symbol of peace rather than that of war is clear.

Sherwood Eddy and Kirby Page identify this with a rejection of a Zealots effort at revolt against Rome by saying, "From his third temptation in the wilderness to the cross of Calvary, Jesus' life and teaching are the absolute antithesis of the spirit and example of the Zealots and the militarists around him. He steadfastly refused to advance his ideals by coercive means."[19]

That Jesus refused to be an earthly ruler and to wage a war of revolt is unquestioned. That the only reason for doing this was a condemnation of warfare is highly questionable. Umphrey Lee

[17]Scott-Craig, *op. cit.*, p. 30.

[18]Cadoux, *op. cit.*, p. 26.

[19]Sherwood Eddy and Kirby Page, *Abolition of War* (New York: George Doubleday Co., 1924), p. 65.

argues that "it is certainly not legitimate to compare ordinary citizens who do not want to fight but who believe that there are circumstances in which it would be justified with wild fanatics of the first century who believed themselves divinely ordained to wade through blood to the domination of the world by a chosen nation."[20]

A more serious objection to that interpretation is that Jesus had a mission of redemption to perform. He would have been sacrificing the very purpose of his life if he had taken the methods of earthly kingship. To read into this rejection simply a condemnation of the war method is to reduce his action to only one aspect of the total temptation experience. Jesus was rejecting not only a method but the whole idea of avoiding the cross.

(2) *The Sermon on the Mount*

In the Sermon on the Mount (Matthew 5-7) Jesus outlines the behavior to be expected of the citizen of his Kingdom. He commands his followers to turn the other cheek when struck with the blow of insult, to go the second mile when one mile is demanded, to love their enemies, and to do to others what they would desire to be done to them. The pacifist sees in all of these injunctions a condemnation of the war method. While a personal orientation is obvious in these commands, these ideas also speak to collective action. John Graham says that all of the qualification of interpretations that might be allowable "cannot make our Lord's teachings mean the exact opposite of what it says."[21] Scott-Craig claims that the command to love the enemy does not just mean personal enemy since the Greek word can also mean public foes.[22]

(3) *Command to Bear Suffering and Overcome Evil With Good*

Paul admonishes Christians to live peaceably with all men, leaving vengeance in the hands of the Lord; Christians are told to overcome evil with good (Romans 12:17-21). Raven sees in

[20]Umphrey Lee, *Historic Church and Modern Pacificism* (New York: Abingdon-Cokesbury Press, 1943), p. 28.

[21]Graham, *op. cit.,* p. 10.

[22]Scott-Craig, *op. cit.,* p. 24.

this idea "the heart of the Christian mystery" in a rejection of the war method.[23] Faunce claims that this saves the pacifist from being a "moral neuter" on vital issues by furnishing a strategy for action.[24]

However, this command cannot be limited to a relationship with the problem of war nor a strategy for pacifist action. Umphrey Lee points this out, saying, "That the principle of overcoming evil with good is creative in Christian ethics is nowhere better shown than in the recognition that this offers a positive method of dealing with evil . . . but one must not read into Paul what is not there. He did not contemplate the substitution of a Christian strategy for the lower but necessary task assigned by God to the powers that be, that of bringing evil men to the book and of staving off the forces of darkness."[25]

Other passages might be dealt with at this point. However, each proof-text comes under the same limitation of reading into the Scriptures a position and a strategy that amounts to a misuse of the Bible in dealing with the question of war and peace.

II. *THE BIBLICAL IDEAL: PEACE AND NONRESISTANCE*

The Bible records the revelation of the way God made His world, His purpose for it, and the principles by which He intends it to operate. While sin has marred and warped His creation at its foundations, the eternal ideals of God still stand in judgment over every scheme and action of man. An examination of the total message of the Bible reveals the spirit as well as the letter of the Scriptures. This examination leads to the inevitable conclusion that God's ideal for his world is peace. Let us examine the content and the nature of these Biblical ideals.

1. Content of the Ideal

(1) *Glimpses of the Ideal in the Old Testament*

In the earlier stages of God's revelation and of Israel's history,

---

[23]Rufus Jones, *The Church, the Gospel, and War* (New York: Harper Bros., 1948), p. 5.

[24]Faunce, *op. cit.*, p. 48.

[25]Lee, *op. cit.*, p. 48.

God commands the nation to wage war. However, even in those days of limited understanding of the nature and purpose of God, there are glimpses of the ideal of peace. The Ten Commandments give as a basic law of God the command, "Thou shalt not kill" (Exodus 20:13). David was denied his dream of constructing a temple for Jehovah because he had been a man of war. God told him, "You have shed much blood and waged great wars; you shall not build a house to my name because you have shed so much blood before me upon the earth. Behold, a son shall be born to you; he shall be a man of peace" (I Chronicles 22:8-9).

The people of Israel were encouraged always to "pray for the peace of Jerusalem" when they went to the house of the Lord (Psalm 122:6). The psalmist sings of the day when this peace with justice will come. He says, "Steadfast love and faithfulness will meet; righteousness and peace will kiss each other" (Psalm 85:10 RSV).

The eighth century prophets, those men with surpassingly marvelous insight into the truths of God, see more clearly the concept of peace. They describe the moral requirements of God with tremendous insight and courage. The words which they speak shine like golden nuggets in the murky streams of many words being spoken about God in their day. One of the most consistent notes they strike is the yearning for the peace which God wills for men.

Isaiah describes the Golden Age when God "shall judge between the nations and shall decide for many peoples. And they shall beat their swords into plowshares and their spears into pruning hooks. Nation shall not lift up sword against nation, neither shall they learn war any more" (Isaiah 2:4). He also perceives that the coming Messiah will be the Prince of Peace (Isaiah 9:6). He predicts that in that day men "shall not hurt or destroy in all my holy mountain" (Isaiah 65:25). The peace about which he speaks will be one in which "Zion shall be redeemed by justice, and those in her who repent, by righteousness" (Isaiah 1:27 RSV).

Micah repeats some of the same promises about the day when men shall learn war no more (Micah 4:3). The yearning for the day of peace runs like a golden thread through each of these prophets.

(2) *Revelation of the Ideal in the New Testament*

While much that is said concerning peace in the New Testament is person-directed rather than nation-directed, the implication of the total message reveals that the desire and will of God is that men live in peace. Jesus is born to the sound of angels proclaiming, "Glory to God in the highest and on earth peace among men with whom he is pleased." (Luke 2:14 RSV). One of the ten blessings Jesus pronounced concerning those in his Kingdom was, "Blessed are the peacemakers for they shall be called the sons of God" (Matthew 5:9). In one of his most beautiful promises Jesus says "Peace I leave with you, my peace I give unto you; not as the world gives do I give to you. Let not your hearts be troubled, neither let them be afraid" (John 14:27). The picture of the Golden Age at the end of time when he returns is one of the conquering king reigning forever and ever in a heaven of peace, with no place for tears and sorrow and death (Revelation 22).

The actual references to peace in the New Testament, however, are not the bases for believing that God's ideal for men is to experience peace. This concept comes from the foundational truths about God which Jesus reveals.

a) God Is a Loving Father

When Christ drew back the curtain to show men the essence of God's nature, he revealed that God is a father and that God is love (Matthew 6:9, I John 4:7-14). He shows that this love is to be reflected in his followers who are commanded to love even their enemies (Matthew 5:44). It is impossible to conceive of the loving Father desiring for men the massive suffering and destruction of warfare. The basic will of God for men must be a peace which not only is characterized by the cessation of hostilities but also by the presence of an active good will overcoming evil.

b) The Worth of the Individual

One of the unique contributions made by the revelation of Christ is the understanding of the infinite worth of every individual human being. In no other ancient religion or philosophy is this concept properly accentuated. This worth centers not in what man is able to produce, nor in his status in life, but in the fact that God loves him. Jesus speaks of God's concern for the sparrow that falls from the sky and tells men that God even numbers the hairs of their heads (Matthew 10:29-31). In this modern day when we are inclined to erase the importance of cities and nations as if they were mere pawns in the struggle for international power, we need to be reminded of Jesus' picture of the heart of God as being like that of a shepherd searching patiently and compassionately in the mountains for one sheep that goes astray (Luke 15).

Whether one agrees with Leyton Richards' strategy of pacificism or not, his summary analysis of the spirit of Christ over against the spirit of war has the ring of truth to it. He says, "That contradiction may be stated in a series of antitheses. The way of war is destructive, of Christ redemptive; war seeks to overcome evil by the infliction of injury upon the evil-doer or his agents, Jesus by enduring the utmost injury that the evil-doer cares to inflict; war treats men as 'things' to be ruthlessly brushed aside, Jesus always treated them as living souls capable of responding to the love of God expressed in his life and death . . . Jesus deliberately lost the battle in order to win men, while war crushes men in order to win the battle."[26]

(3) *Nonresistance*

A careful reading of the New Testament produces the impression that the ideal of Christ is not only peace but also nonresistance. Nonresistance is essentially different from the pacificism of today which majors on the idea of nonviolence. Reinhold Niebuhr flatly declares that "there is not the slightest support in

[26]Leyton Richards, *Christian Pacificism After Two World Wars* (London: Independent Press, Ltd., 1948), p. 30.

scripture for this doctrine of nonviolence."[27] Umphrey Lee agrees, saying, "But nonviolent resistance, non-cooperation, by whatever name called, is a technique to secure political power, to secure material possessions. To see in these a carrying-out of one of our Lord's counsels is to misread all that he said."[28]

The example of Jesus is not nonviolence, it is nonresistance. He refused to resist his own enemies. He commands his followers to love one another even as he had loved them and to love their enemies (John 13:34, Matthew 5:44). He speaks in terms of *agape* love which is a self-forgetting kind of love. The absence of hate is not the presence of this kind of love. It is an active love which moves to reconciliation. The Christian is commanded by Paul not to seek vengeance in any fashion (Romans 12:17-21). Jesus says that the use of force will mean the increase of a harvest of destruction so that they who live by the sword will die by the sword (Matthew 26:52). The spirit of nonvindictiveness permeates all of the New Testament.

2. The Nature of Biblical Ideals

Since the content of the Biblical ideal is peace and nonresistance motivated by active good will, it is wise for us to examine the nature of Biblical ideals. These ideals can be of great practical help to us in a warring and sinful world.

It is the nature of Biblical ideals to be absolute. They move in harmony with the eternal plan of God and do not take into account the complexities of a warped world nor the weakness of human abilities. They provide no exceptions nor loopholes. Though Christians are assured grace and forgiveness, these ideals serve as magnets toward which we are attracted rather than totally attainable goals. For instance, Jesus commanded men to be perfect even as the Father in heaven is perfect (Matthew 5:48). Though each man knows that he cannot be as perfect or complete as God, this is his goal. He did not say be almost perfect because each man would crowd into the word "almost" each of his own weaknesses or sins. The goal is absolute.

---

[27]Niebuhr, *op. cit.*, p. 10.
[28]Lee, *op. cit.*, p. 27.

It is especially important to understand the nature of Biblical idealism in dealing with the concept of peace. The Christian in a warped and sinful world confronts the dilemma of conflicting values. Grievous injustice exists in our world. The same *agape* principle which calls for peace also evokes the response of sympathy for the victims of injustice. The question of resisting evil-doers for the protection not of self but of others challenges Christian thinking. When does peace become appeasement? The Bible provides no blueprint for the behavior of the Christian in the presence of these conflicting responsibilities. The Biblical ideal must be a magnetic pole by which our compasses are set, so that we make our decisions in the light of them. Complete fulfillment of these ideals awaits the perfect world which God will bring to pass in the final day.

III. *THE SEARCH FOR A CHRISTIAN POSTURE IN A WARRING WORLD*

It is now in order for us to turn our attention to the practical meaning of these Biblical teachings concerning the concept of peace. What is the answer to the quest for a Christian posture in our warring world? Conflicting ideologies, national interests, economic interests, racial attitudes, and wills to power make our world a kaleidoscope of complex issues. Each day seems to bring new patterns for international problems. How can one make his path straight in the tangled mass of a complex world?

Basic to the search for a Christian posture should be an understanding of our human limitations. Humility must characterize Christians in the search for answers to these hard questions. We are not omniscient. Most of us are not technological experts in the weaponry of our day. We certainly want to be informed citizens, but we must recognize that we are limited in much of the detailed information which is available to policy-makers. Therefore, many of our conclusions must be under constant re-evaluation in the light of new information. Implied in this is an unwillingness to pass too quick a judgment upon the posture and opinion of differing brethren in Christ.

While we must confess our limitations, we should not evade the responsibility of thinking through the things which make for peace from a sincere and alert Christian perspective. We need to be committed to the search for a Christian position.

Let us then examine three of the basic positions most American Christians are now assuming.

1. The "Patriot" Posture or the "Holy War" Position

The first one may be termed the "patriot" posture. The basic assumption of a certain kind of self-styled patriot is summed up in Al Capp's caricature of the slogan of one of the nation's giant business enterprises, "What's good for General Bullmoose is good for everybody." Certainly what is best for the highest and broadest interpretation of the national interest is best for the world because our national destiny is tied to the search for peace with justice for the nations of the world. However, the undiscerning person who justifies all questions simply on the level of narrow nationalism tends to ignore the Biblical ideal of peace even as an influential factor in his thinking.

This kind of position tends also to ignore the wearying complexities of our international situation in favor of a simple "shoot the bad guys" solution. The thought seldom occurs that there is a grave problem in determining who the "bad guys" are. The grim result of precipitating nuclear war does not seem to faze these super-patriots.

There is something appealing about this position because it is the easiest one to hold. No tensions or frustrations are created. That is, there are no tensions or frustrations unless one examines the lessons of history and finds the near-sighted men of the pulpits of yesterday searching the Scriptures to justify their national policies and then goes on to discover that time has proven them false prophets, so shaped by their culture that they did not discern the mind of God.

Loyalty to one's nation is an essential ingredient of alert Christian citizenship. The highest kind of loyalty one can bring to his nation is to be bringing constantly to bear upon its decisions the best of Christian insights about Biblical ideals.

2. The Pacifist Posture or the "No War" Position

There are those Christians who read the Bible and become convinced that their position must be one of refusal to take human life under any circumstances. These may vary from the nonresister to the nonviolent resister.

Far too often in Christian history and in more recent experience these men are discredited in the public mind under the stigma of being soft or cowardly. While some may hide cowardice under a cloak of pacificism, the true pacificist is anything but a coward. He has chosen a lonely position out of his conviction and is usually willing to demonstrate physical courage in the task of saving lives. He simply cannot reconcile his Biblical understanding of the demands of Christ with the taking of life.

There are some defects in the pacifist posture which may be noted. Persons who hold this position often fail to see that they also have adopted a compromising position. Identifying the total message of the Gospel with the idea of the sanctity of life, they fail to see that they have chosen not to oppose tyranny and not to accept the responsibility for establishing justice on earth.

There is also a tendency to defend pacificism as a practical strategy in international affairs. The plea centers in the idea that if every one would follow this method, the problem of international conflict would be solved. The thesis is that God would provide a special immunity from disaster for the nation which showed itself worthy by renouncing violence. Niebuhr answers this argument by saying, "Actually the historical process is not so simply moral. Nations as well as individuals may be destroyed not only by violating the laws of life, but also by achieving a defenseless purity, incompatible with the necessities of survival. Ultimately New Testament faith was to revere a Christ whose perfect goodness was validated by an obvious defeat in history. But there are Christian perfectionists who still do not understand the logic of the cross. They hope that if goodness is only perfect enough its triumph in history will be assured."[29]

[29]Reinhold Niebuhr, *Faith and History* (New York: Charles Scribner's Sons, 1949), p. 128.

A third defect in this posture is the tendency to identify nonviolence with nonresistance as the ideal of Christ. Nonviolent resistance is a form of warfare. While there are occasions, such as in the present racial crisis, in which it is a closer approximation to the ideal of Christian love than other forms of protest, it still stands under the judgment of the ideal of love. To miss this fact is to miss the challenge of the Biblical ideal.

There are genuine contributions to be made by the person assuming the pacificist posture from personal conviction. If he is under no illusions about the practicality of his position as it relates to resisting injustice and formulating solutions to international policy, he is in the position to witness to a truth about God and the way God wants his world to be. He can be a constant reminder to those who do not agree with his position that they should never feel entirely at home with their accommodations to an evil world. To the degree that he contributes to the uneasiness of conscience of the Christians who have come to feel at home in a warring world, he makes an essential witness for Christ. In the final analysis one of the essential ingredients of the *koinonia* fellowship of Christians is that we contribute to each other our insights about God, thus keeping ourselves in constant tension with the Christian ideal, which tension is essential to our being effective as the salt of the earth.

3. The Accommodationist Posture or the "Just War" Position

The third posture which Christians are adopting within a warring world is that of accommodation. This position allows a full appreciation for the concept of peace and the idea of nonresistance as ideals toward which we should be constantly kept in tension. It takes into account the fact that we are in a sinful world which is not ready for the ideal of Christ. It then allows one to move into the practical decisions of a warring world in attempting to bring each one of them under the judgment of the ideal of love and the reflection of that ideal in the arrangements of justice.

This accommodation may gravitate to various levels. Some would justify warfare for the nation with the highest degree of justice in its cause. Some shrink from the terminology of "just war" because of the realization that pure justice is exceedingly scarce in the brutalities of modern international life.

The nuclear pacifist holds the accommodationist position as do those who would justify the use of nuclear weaponry.

There are defects in this position. It is always tempting to accept this reasoning because the tides of public opinion move one along with it. Accommodation easily becomes compromise when one's conscience becomes desensitized. The accommodation can easily deteriorate into a calculation ethic which finally results in a justifying of brutal behavior patterns totally unworthy of the Christians. For instance, in a recent conference discussion with Dr. Ernest LeFever of the Department of Defense Analysis (author of the book *Ethics and Foreign Policy*) this ethic of calculation centered on a discussion of guerrilla warfare. The problem concerned a captured guerrilla who might have information about an attack. Securing of this information would mean a possibility of saving fifty lives. On this basis, torturing this man was considered justifiable Christian behavior. The danger of this kind of reasoning is that the means so affect the end result that the persons doing the torturing become just like the enemies whom they are trying to conquer.

The point is that the accommodationist must be ever alert to the ideals of Christ and seek to be as close to them as possible within the actual situation.

As a practical matter this will mean support for every worthy effort to achieve peace with justice in our world. It will mean support for current moves to develop weapons which will allow a policy of international confrontation short of dependence upon nuclear warfare. It will mean that Christians will pray for peace, not with the perfunctory attitude of routine duty but with the desperate intercession of men who yearn to see the will of God done in our warped world.

CONCLUSION

In conclusion, there are kindled two impressions from the study of the Bible's teachings concerning war and peace. The first is the realization that Christians should be extremely hesitant to be judgmental toward other Christians who reach conclusions different from their own regarding this complex question. Christians should rather serve in witnessing to each other in love concerning insights into the mind of Christ about this critical matter. The other impression is a stirring of a deeper yearning for the day when the kingdoms of this world become the kingdom of our Lord Christ.

3.

A HISTORICAL VIEW OF CHRISTIANS AND PEACE

William M. Pinson, Jr.
Associate Professor of Christian Ethics
Southwestern Baptist Theological Seminary
Fort Worth, Texas

In the United States, the almost fatalistic acceptance of war combined with the general attitude that anyone who zealously advocates peace is a "pink" has all but silenced a prophetic Christian witness about war and peace. While the expanding welfare state in this country has been bitterly denounced by many, the expanding warfare state has generally been accepted. War movies, television combat shows, weapon advertisements in magazines, military enlistment displays in stores and post offices, flights of military planes overhead, and military convoys on highways are ever present but seldom questioned. Apparently, the constant presence of the warfare state has dulled Christian consciences. Most Christian consciences seem little troubled by problems of war and peace.

For example, seminary students who work in defense plants apparently are little troubled by the seeming inconsistency of making instruments of war to earn money to obtain an education about the Prince of Peace.

Many Christians who volunteer for military service never ask the One to whom they owe primary allegiance, "Lord, what would *you* have me do?"

Ministers have been known to enter the military chaplaincy without giving serious thought to the question of war and the Christian conscience.

Many Christians who are incensed when a drunk slaughters a respectable family in an automobile accident appear to have experienced no troubling of conscience at the incineration of tens of thousands of nonmilitary, respectable citizens in the atomic blasts of Hiroshima and Nagasaki and the obliteration bombing of Hamburg and Berlin.

Aside from numerous platitudes on peace often approved by religious conventions, the Christian community in the United States has done little in recent years to talk down war and talk up peace. This has not always been true. In the past, many Christians have given themselves to strenuous thought and have taken courageous stands in regard to war and peace. The purpose now is to examine what these Christians have said and done.

Pre-Christian Period

The history of thought on peace begins prior to the Christian movement. Roland Bainton, in his excellent book, *Christian Attitudes Toward War and Peace*, points out that among all ancient peoples, except perhaps the Assyrians, peace was the ideal.[1] While ancient epics glorify national war heroes, war for the ancients was generally regarded as a tragic interruption of ordinary life. Peace was especially revered by the civilizations which form the basis of our own—the Hebrew, Greek, and Roman.

For the Hebrews, peace was more than the absence of war. It was the gift of God and involved not only cessation of military combat, but also national well-being and prosperity. For the Greeks, peace was a state of order and coherence which made for a pleasant life. For the Romans, peace was essentially the absence of war made possible by pacts or agreements between

---

[1]*Christian Attitudes Toward War and Peace,* (New York: Abingdon Press, 1960), pp. 17-32. This book provided the basic material for this introductory section and is one of the best books available on the history of Christian thought in regard to war and peace.

nations. Though noted for their military genius, the Romans considered their greatest accomplishment to be the *Pax Romana*, the Peace of Rome.

While peace was considered by the ancients to be the ideal relationship between peoples, it was not considered the highest good. Other things were treasured more highly than peace—justice, freedom, honor, material possessions, national existence. Where these were threatened, war was justified. Some, especially the Hebrews, fought religious wars or crusades; the only justification usually given for such a war was that the god of the people had commanded it. Pacifism was extremely rare among ancient peoples.

Most of the concepts held by Christians about war and peace did not have their genesis in the Christian movement. The concepts originated with pre-Christian civilizations and were accommodated to the Christian faith. Christians, therefore, as those in pre-Christian times, have agreed that peace is the ideal relationship between states and peoples. Beyond this, however, there has been little agreement. Some Christians have approved "just" wars and even crusades, while others have condemned all wars.

Early Period (30-300 A.D.)

During the early years of the Christian movement, pacifism prevailed. Not until 183 A.D. is there any record of Christians serving with the military. "From the end of the New Testament period to the decade 170-180 A.D., there is no evidence whatever of Christians in the army."[2] During this same period, there was little said by Christian writers on the subject of war and peace.[3] Therefore, it is difficult to determine why Christians were not in the army. Their absence can be explained in one of two ways:

---

[2]*Ibid.*, p. 67.

[3]T. B. Maston, ***Christianity and World Issues,*** (New York: The Macmillan Company, 1957), p. 248. Justin Martyr was seemingly the first Christian to make an explicit statement on war and peace. About 150 A.D. he wrote, "We who delighted in war, in the slaughter of one another, and in every other kind of iniquity have in every part of the world converted our weapons of war into implements of peace."

(1) They were disqualified by the government, or (2) they had convictions against serving in the army. It is not necessarily true that the conviction was based on a belief that war is wrong. For example, refusal to participate in the military could have been based on a fear of idolatry since soldiers had to pledge their primary allegiance to Caesar. Nevertheless, many scholars are convinced that the early Christians did not participate in military life because they were pacifist by conviction.

Between 200-300 A.D. the silence on war was broken. As more and more Christians entered military service, Christian writers spoke out against war and warned Christians not to become involved in the military. Roland Bainton states that "all of the outstanding writers of the East and West (from 200-300 A.D.) repudiated participation in warfare for Christians."[4]

Clement of Alexandria said, "In peace, not in war, we are trained." Tertullian in his *Apology* declared, "Christ in disarming Peter ungirt every soldier." Cyprian insisted that iron was designed by God for tilling, not killing. Lactantius "suggested that since God prohibited killing it was not lawful for a 'just man' to serve as a soldier."[5]

The opposition of the early church leaders to war was based in the main on two reasons: (1) War involves taking human life which is contrary to the commandment of God and contrary to the Christian spirit. (2) The conduct of soldiers, even in peace time, is unbecoming for a Christian.

During the fourth century, the Christian attitude toward war changed drastically. C. J. Cadoux, renowned historian of the early church period, has written, "The church as a whole definitely gave up her anti-militarist leanings, abandoned all her scruples, finally adopted the imperial point of view, and treated the ethical problem involved as a closed question."[6]

The cross, once a symbol of the Christian's willingness to die

---

[4]Bainton, *op. cit.*, p. 73.

[5]Maston, *op. cit.*, p. 250.

[6]C. J. Cadoux, *The Early Christian Attitude to War* (London: Headley Brothers Publishers, Ltd., 1919), p. 256.

rather than compromise principle, became an ensign of the military. The church leader, Ambrose, declared, "Not eagles and birds must lead the army, but thy name and religion, O Jesus."

Christians were urged to participate in war. Athanasius, the "Father of Orthodoxy," stated that it was not only lawful but praiseworthy to kill enemies in war. In 314 A.D., the Synod of Arelate enacted a canon which apparently threatened with excommunication Christian soldiers who insisted on quitting the army. By 416 A.D., the situation had been so altered that non-Christians were forbidden to serve in the army!

Why did such a great change occur in such a short time? Apparently, the chief reason why the church came to advocate war was that the church made peace with the world. When the church entered into its unholy alliance with the state under Constantine, it took on many of the attitudes of the state. When Christianity became the state religion, in return for favors from the state, the church gave its blessing and support to activities of the state, including war.

Middle Ages (400-1500 A.D.)

During the Middle Ages, the main stream of the Christian movement not only continued to lend its approval to war but also became even more deeply involved in war. The Roman Catholic Church gave its approval to the feudal system which was essentially a system of perpetual war. The Roman Catholic Church also encouraged and backed the Crusades, the first great religious wars fought by Christians. The Crusades were wars initiated by the Roman Catholic Church against the Moslems. The expressed purpose of the Crusades was to place control of the Holy Land in Christian hands, and interestingly enough, to bring peace to Europe by directing bellicosity to a foreign adventure. These wars were as cruel and bloody as any war by a secular power. All of the refinements and restrictions which had been developed by the Roman Catholic Church were removed when the enemy was the infidel. The account of Jerusalem's capture by the Crusaders, by one who participated in the battle, is indicative of the attitude of the Christian warriors:

> Piles of heads, hands, and feet were to be seen in the streets of the city . . . in the temple and portico of Solomon, men rode in blood up to their knees and the bridle reins. Indeed, it was a just and splendid judgment of God . . . This day, I say, will be famous in all future ages, for it turned our labors and sorrows into joy and exultation; this day, I say, marks the justification of all Christianity.[7]

The crusade-type war was also unleashed by the Roman Catholic Church on sects considered heretical. The bloodiest crusades were against the Cathari in southern France. The Crusaders attacked cities—hanging, beheading, burning—all "with unspeakable joy." There was utter contempt for human life. When a Papal legate in charge of one of the battles was asked how to distinguish between the Cathari and the Catholics, he replied, "Kill them all; God will know which are His."

The Middle Ages was not devoid of a witness for peace, however. Monks and priests were exempt from military service. It was felt that war polluted men's lives and that holy men should be spared such pollution. For the most part, monastics and clerics abstained from war. There were exceptions. A few monastic military orders were formed, such as the Templars and Hospitalers. At times, church leaders participated in the combat. Even then, there is evidence that they had troubled consciences concerning their fighting. For example, in 1182 A.D., the Archbishop of Mainz killed nine men in battle. However, he was careful to beat them to death with a club, rather than killing them with a sword, because the church abhorred the shedding of blood! In spite of a number of battling bishops and combative cardinals, the clergy for the most part did not fight but served as a witness, however ineffective, that war is not God's ideal.

Perhaps the best indication of the church's troubled conscience over its approval of war was the numerous efforts by church leaders to justify the church's position and to refine the practice of

---

[7]Bainton, *op. cit.*, p. 112.

war. Two theologians who discussed war extensively were Augustine (354-430 A.D.) and Thomas Aquinas (1224-1274 A.D.). Augustine, who seemed to have had an uneasy conscience concerning the church's approval of war, insisted that the only kind of wars which should be waged are Just Wars. He felt that despite the evil of war, war may at times be necessary and may serve a useful purpose. Thomas agreed with Augustine and elaborated on his theory of Just War. According to Thomas Aquinas, a Just War has at least three characteristics: (1) It is waged by a sovereign government, not by individuals. (2) It must be for a just cause. (3) Those who carry on the war must have good intentions; they must desire to promote good or hinder evil.

Through emphasizing the Just War, church leaders endeavored to curb war and promote peace. Two other concepts were promoted by church officials to curtail fighting—the Peace of God and the Truce of God. The Peace of God limited those who could be involved in war. One effort in the Middle Ages to gain more peace was to expand the number of those who were excluded from war. The Council of Narbonne in 1054, for example, decreed that there should be no attack on the following persons: clerics, monks, nuns, women, pilgrims, merchants, peasants, visitors to councils, or shepherds.

The Truce of God limited the time for military operations. "There was to be no fighting from Advent through Epiphany nor from Septuagesima until the eighth day after Pentecost, nor on Sundays, Fridays, and every one of the holy days throughout the year."[8] Of course, it was practically impossible to enforce the Peace of God and Truce of God and they were largely ineffectual. Yet, they did demonstrate Christian concern for peace.

The most consistent exponents of peace were not found in the Roman Catholic Church, however, but in the many sects which arose in the late Middle Ages. On the whole, the Waldensians, Franciscan Tertiaries, and Cathari were pacifist. The reasons for

[8] *Ibid.*, p. 110.

their pacifism were varied. The Cathari, for example, believed in transmigration of souls and for that reason were opposed to the taking of life. Of necessity, therefore, they rejected war, though when attacked they defended themselves.

One branch of the Hussite movement was strongly pacifist. The outstanding leader of this group was Peter Chelciky, who scathed those who scrupled to eat swine flesh on Friday but not to shed human blood. His reasons for pacifism were convincing —that the first age of the church was the golden age and this age was pacificist; that the mission of the church was to redeem souls, not destroy bodies; that the law of Christ was love which forbids killing. Chelciky taught that the state existed only to restrain sin and that the government should be administered by sinners. Therefore, Christians should refuse military or public positions.

Reformation (1500-1700)

The Reformation brought little that was new in regard to Christian thought and action pertaining to war and peace. All three of the main positions on war—Pacifism, the Just War, the Crusade—were taken by those who maintained an existence separate from the Roman Catholic Church during the Reformation period.

The theory of the Just War was adopted by Martin Luther. He felt that some types of war could be justified. Luther believed that wars could be used to promote peace and protect good. Martin Luther taught that Christians should fight in wars when called into service by a ruler whose cause is right. He did not, however, give his blanket approval to Christian participation in war. A Christian was not to fight under the following circumstances: when the war was over a religious question, when the war was a war of aggression, when the war was against a superior, or when the Christian's ruler was in the wrong. Luther also insisted that pastors should not fight.

The Reformer instructed Christian soldiers to fight ferociously, but without greed and evil thoughts. Christian soldiers, in the words of Luther, were to "smite, stab, slay, and kill." They were to remember, however, that they fought as citizens, not as Christians.

John Calvin had less to say about war than Luther. He justified certain kinds of war using as his authority the Old Testament, but he had no elaborate system as did Augustine, Aquinas, and Luther. Ernst Troeltsch summarizes Calvin's position as follows:

> War, he held, is a matter which concerns the state, which is permitted to use it for the secular purposes of defense, provided that it is waged with no confidence in the arm of flesh and with trust in God in all humility and Christian austerity of morals.[9]

Calvin's testimony for peace was not noteworthy. He did urge that disputes be settled without recourse to arms if possible and stated that the purpose of war should be to restore peace.

The followers of Calvin waged holy wars—crusades—on the Continent and in Scotland and England. Calvin produced in his followers little conscience in regard to war. His disciples participated enthusiastically in the Wars of Religion which followed the initial stage of the Reformation. These wars, fought in the name of Christianity, were exceedingly cruel. Huguenots, for example, wore strings of priests' ears and buried Catholics to their necks and played ninepins with their heads.

The most consistent advocates of peace during the Reformation period were sects such as the Quakers, Mennonites, and certain of the Anabaptists. Their views were expressed in "detachment from the State, from all official positions; from law, force, and the oath; and from war, violence, and capital punishment."[10] Believing that they should live according to the teachings of the Sermon on the Mount and believing that this is impossible if one accepts the ways of society, they detached themselves from society. Strongly emphasizing love, they renounced war which they felt to be contrary to love.

---

[9]Ernst Troeltsch, *The Social Teaching of the Christian Churches* (New York: Harper and Brothers, Harper Torchbooks, 1960, II), p. 651.

[10]*Ibid.*, p. 696.

The Anabaptists were severely persecuted by both Roman Catholics and Protestants. Amidst the confusion of persecution, the Baptist groups became diversified in belief. On the Continent, Menno Simons gathered a group of Anabaptists into a peaceful community. With this began the Mennonite movement which strongly forbade participation in war. As the Baptist movement swept into England, however, it lost much of its pacifist tendencies. Baptist churches in England permitted their members to take part in wars. Baptists were especially active in the army of Cromwell and were excellent troops.

The Quakers in many ways were similar to the early Anabaptist groups. However, they put much emphasis on their concept of the inner light. Quakers believed that a person should live up to the light he had. If a man believed in fighting a just war, he should fight. Quakers believed, however, that as a man gained more of the light, he would become a pacifist. Quakers rather consistently refused to take an active part in war. In some instances, such as in Pennsylvania, their refusal to become involved in war cost them political position and power.

Pacifist Quakers have not always been as anxious to avoid the appearance of war as some suppose. One Quaker who operated a merchant ship mounted huge wooden cannons on his ship to frighten away pirates. Such happenings indicate that the story about the Quaker who said to a burglar he had caught, "Friend, I would do thee no harm, but thou art standing where I am about to shoot," may have some basis in fact.

It should be understood that pacifism is not a simple concept. Many degrees of pacifism and many bases for pacifism have been expressed by Christians. For example, some who claim to be pacifists condemn all use of force, whether by the police or by an army. Others recognize police power, but not armies. Some pacifists simply base their position on biblical passages. Others base theirs on a rational argument: war is senseless and the best way to eliminate it is not to participate in it. Some pacifists believe that pacifism is the surest way to overcome a foe; others insist that pacifism may not overcome the enemy but that Christians should be pacifist so that in suffering they will bear witness of love for their fellow man.

A review of the Reformation Period would not be complete without mention of the wars of conquest which took place in the New World during this period. The Spanish conquistadores swept across South America in the name of Christ—burning, killing, torturing, raping, plundering under the sign of the cross. Few Christians protested. The priest Las Casas pled for peaceful conversion of the natives, but in vain. In the North, conquest was less swift and bloody but not without cruel wars. Again, few Christian voices were raised in protest. John Elliot and David Brainard pleaded for peace and humane treatment of the Indians, and the Quakers generally lived in peace with the natives. But these were exceptions.

Modern Period (1600-Present)

The cruel Wars of Religion came to a close in the eighteenth century. People now found religious wars repulsive. War again became more or less a game involving mercenaries and not civilians. Restraint was used in battle. Revolutions were a significant part of the eighteenth-century war picture, among them being our own American Revolution.

In the colonies, little was said about peace during the Revolution. The churches, in general, supported the war effort. Both Washington and Jefferson took special notice of the Baptist contribution to the Revolution. The traditional pacifist groups, such as the Quakers and Mennonites, did not actively support either side in the Revolution. The clergy of the Episcopal and Methodist churches in general sided with England or remained neutral, but the laymen of these churches were active revolutionaries.

In the nineteenth century, the bloodiest single war was the Civil War in the United States. Churches in the North and in the South sided with their respective governments and claimed the blessings of God for their cause. The Quakers, who had led in the move to abolish slavery, were caught in a dilemma. The North was fighting primarily to save the Union, but also to free the slaves. The Quakers favored abolition, but they opposed war. Generally, they remained pacifist but their sympathies were with the North.

Southern Baptists, on the other hand, gave their wholehearted approval to the Confederacy. Baptists furnished more troops than did any other group to the Confederate armies. Peace was foreign to the Baptist spirit in the South. In the 1861 meeting of the Southern Baptist Convention, the messengers condemned Northern politicians and churchmen for forcing war on the South. If any pro-Union or pro-peace sentiment was expressed at the Convention, it is not evident in the records.

Baptists in Virginia appealed "to the God of Battles for help in this hour of darkness and peril."[11] Baptists in Louisiana united in a prayer of thanksgiving for the success of Confederate arms after the first year of conflict.[12] As the Confederate armies began to suffer reverses, Baptist sentiment remained belligerent. In 1863, the Southern Baptist Convention declared, "While deploring the dreadful evils of the war, and earnestly desiring peace, we have no thought of ever yielding."[13] The same Convention stated, "The events of the past two years have only confirmed the conviction . . . that the war which has been forced upon us is, on our part, just and necessary." Because Southern Baptists believed so fervently that the war they supported was a just war, they had great difficulty in adjusting to defeat.[14]

In addition to the Civil War, the United States fought three other wars in the nineteenth century—in 1812 with England, in 1845 with Mexico, and in 1898 with Spain. While little is known about the Baptist reaction in 1812, Southern Baptists were particularly strong in their support of the other two wars. They justified them mainly on the grounds of bringing religious liberty

[11] *Minutes of the Baptist General Association of Virginia,* 1861, p. 16.
[12] *Louisiana Baptist State Convention Minutes,* 1862, pp. 10-11.
[13] *Southern Baptist Convention Minutes,* 1863, p. 54.
[14] For an excellent discussion on Baptists and the peace following the war, see Rufus Spain, "Attitudes and Reactions of Southern Baptists to Certain Problems of Society, 1865-1900," a Ph.D. dissertation at Vanderbilt University, 1961, pp. 32-43.

to oppressed peoples and opening new areas for mission work. In 1899, for example, the Southern Baptist Convention gave thanks for the freedom gained by Cubans and for the opening of the country to extensive missionary work.[15]

In the world as a whole, the nineteenth century was a time of relative peace. Hope was high that war could be abolished. Many peace societies were formed. Although the churches did not play a direct role in most of the peace efforts, for the most part they furnished inspiration for the peace movement and supported it.

In the twentieth century, churches have become very vocal on war and peace. The twentieth century has seen the return of all-out war on a world-wide scale. World War I and World War II were the most extensive and bloodiest wars ever fought. During World War I, the churches on both sides of the conflict supported their respective governments. In America, only the traditional pacifist groups and a few other churchmen remained pacifist. Both the Allies and the Central Powers claimed the blessing of God for their cause. The war was something of a holy crusade. In the United States, Jesus was dressed in khaki and portrayed as sighting down a gun barrel. To kill Germans was to purge the world of monsters. In 1917, in a sermon in Washington, D. C., a minister said, "It is God who has summoned us to this war. It is His war we are fighting . . . the greatest in history—the holiest. It is in the profoundest and truest sense a Holy War." At the same time, German troops went into battle with "God Be With Us" stamped on their belt buckles and helmets, and shouted as their motto, "For God and Fatherland."

With the coming of World War I, Baptist statements in favor of peace suddenly ceased. In 1917, the messengers of the Southern Baptist Convention refused to pass a motion which deplored the war.[16] A special report on the world crisis to the same Convention painted the picture as morally black and white. The re-

[15] *Southern Baptist Convention Annual*, 1899, pp. 38-39.
[16] *Southern Baptist Convention Annual*, 1917, p. 74.

port states, "We recognize (the war) as a struggle of militarism, autocracy, and special privilege against the simple fundamental, indefeasible and inalienable human rights."[17]

By 1918, the war had become a holy crusade. During the Convention of that year, Baptists were challenged to overcome "the hateful menace of German domination of the world." They were told, "The issues at stake are not primarily personal or political. They are in essence religious. They are concerned with fundamental human rights and liberties . . . There must be no limit to the ardor and completeness of our devotion."[18] In 1919, the president of the Southern Baptist Convention praised the war not only for freeing oppressed people but also for cutting down liquor consumption and prostitution.[19]

Following World War I, churchmen had second thoughts about their all-out support of the war. Many expressed regret that they had supported the war effort and pledged themselves to a pacifist position. Especially in England and the United States a great peace wave swept the churches.

The peace movement did not die easily. Even when war with anti-Christian powers seemed unavoidable, many church leaders in this country and England remained pacifist. When war finally came, the churches—as usual—fell in line to support their government in the conflict. But the church's support, unlike that during World War I, was not enthusiastic. One minister said, "This is the saddest war in history. We are not jubilant, but infinitely dejected. We expect nothing from this war except that everything sweet and precious will be crushed out of life for most of us. Nevertheless, we could do no other."[20] Men who had pledged themselves to a pacifist position reluctantly changed their minds. One said, "I used to be a pacifist. I know now that I would rather go to hell for fighting than have my son brought up to think that

[17]*Ibid.*, p. 102.
[18]*Southern Baptist Convention Annual*, 1918, pp. 73-74.
[19]*Southern Baptist Convention Annual*, 1919, p. 17.
[20]Bainton, *op. cit.*, p. 221.
[21]*Ibid.*, p. 218.

it was funny to kick a Jew in the stomach."[21] Only approximately twelve thousand conscientious objectors stood firm in their pacifist position.

With the cessation of conflict, another wave of pacifism swept the Western world. But it was not so idealistic as that of the 1930's, and it was short-lived. The peace following World War II has been an uneasy peace. Numerous limited wars have been fought since 1945. The Cold War and the Communist peace line have caused Christian statements on peace to be muted and Christian thinking to be confused. The churches, however, have not been silent on peace. In the United States, most church groups periodically pass resolutions or issue statements condemning war and commending peace. A few Christian leaders have given considerable attention to the problem of peace, among them being Reinhold Niebuhr, Paul Ramsey, Roland Bainton, Charles Wells, and Culbert Rutenber.

Summary

During the first two centuries of its existence, the Christian movement was pacifist. When the church made peace with the world and allied itself with the state, Christians began to give approval to war. Just War was, in general, approved. Elaborate theories of what made a war "just" were developed by Christian thinkers such as Augustine, Aquinas, and Luther. During the Middle Ages, the Roman Catholic Church went to war in the Crusades.

These three practices—Pacifism, Just War, Crusade—in regard to war continue to be expressed. In the twentieth century, World War I took the form of a Crusade. World War II was considered a Just War. The intervening years saw a rise in pacifist sentiment. Today, a pacifist position is held by only a few. Most pacifists are Quakers or Mennonites but some pacifists are to be found scattered among the other denominations or in no religious group at all. Most Christians hold some form of the Just War theory. Christians have, in general, had more to do with war than with peace.

In the main, Christians have spoken for peace. In periods of war, however, they have given their support to war. It is not surprising, therefore, that in this present war called peace, Christians are sounding an uncertain note on the subject of peace.

In a time when the atomic bomb threatens to end the Atomic Age, we can no longer afford the luxury of an ostrich-like stance. Our ignoring the specter of war will not cause it to go away. We must learn hard lessons from the disheartening story of the relationship of Christians to war in the past and give ourselves to grappling with the dangerous issues of the present. To paraphrase a part of Romans 13 from Phillips' translation, Paul might say to this twentieth century world of war, "It is high time to awake out of our sleep in regard to war and peace. The night of cold war terror is far spent. The synthetic day from the blast of atomic weapons is at hand. Let us, therefore, cast off the works of war and let us put on the ways of peace."

4.

THE IMPERATIVE OF PEACE IN A NUCLEAR AGE

CHARLES WELLBORN
Chaplain
Florida State University
Tallahassee, Florida

In a recent issue of the *Saturday Review,* Marshall Fishwick begins an essay by quoting the words of the Angel Gabriel in Marc Connally's dramatic masterpiece, *Green Pastures.* Looking down from heaven on the chaos and confusion of earth, Gabriel observes sadly, "Everything nailed down is coming loose."[1]

If those words were appropriate in the days of 1930, when the play first appeared, how much more fitting they are today! The times of the Great Depression were trying, but, as Fishwick also comments, when we compare the problems of the Thirties with those of the Sixties, we ". . . tend to agree with the harassed executive in a recent *New Yorker* cartoon who gazed out of the window and murmured: 'Oh, for the good old days when all we had to fear was fear itself.' "[2]

Today we stand, in Secretary of State Dean Rusk's gripping phrase, "eyeball to eyeball" with our atomic adversaries, knowing that the blowup may come at any moment. As for what will happen when it does come, the dimensions of that problem have long

[1]Marshall Fishwick, "Everything Nailed Down Is Coming Loose," *Saturday Review* (June 29, 1963), p. 11.
[2]*Ibid.,* p. 11.

ago exhausted the resources of ordinary language. A new and ponderous terminology, rivaling the most complicated productions of medieval theologians, spouts steadily from the professional theorists on nuclear warfare. We are told of "spasm response," "second strike counterforce capability," "unlimited counter-city retaliation," and "counterforce plus bonus civilian damage." In order to reduce estimates of possible nuclear casualties to manageable terms, Pentagon spokesmen now talk in terms of "megacorpses," a convenient and thoroughly dreadful expression which, in a computer age, neatly represents a million dead human beings. Thus, we reach a new high in the art of the utterly impersonal. It is this kind of impersonal thinking, incidentally, which helps to delude some people into believing that our national policy can successfully consist of "throwing our weight around," saber rattling, waving a big stick, and, generally, telling the rest of the world to behave our way, or else.

But man has strained the resources not only of his language. We have rapidly approached the outer limits of human thought and imagination. Herman Kahn, whose earlier book, called *On Thermonuclear War,* is a sort of controversial classic in the field of Strategics, the theory of atomic warfare, chose as the title of his more recent volume: *Thinking About the Unthinkable.* Mr. Kahn is the man to whom we are indebted for the edifying concept of the "Doomsday Machine," the ideal method of massive deterrence in international policy. Under this system, each nation, large or small, would be equipped with a machine capable of blowing the earth to pieces. Such a machine is thoroughly practical, contends Kahn, and can now be built at a cost of between fifty and a hundred billion dollars. Each machine would be set to go off automatically in case of any enemy attack. Is it any wonder that total destruction, scientifically calculated in such dollar-and-cents terms, tends to leap the boundaries of human sanity? The problem forces men like Dr. Paul Ramsay of Princeton University to try to distinguish between the "unthinkable" and the "un-do-able," with the thesis that certain actions, such as the total destruction of the human race, are not only unthinkable; they are morally and psychologically "un-do-able."

What is most clear is the hard fact that the time has come when the unthinkable, the "un-do-able," and the inexpressible must somehow be faced and dealt with by ordinary human beings. As Albert Einstein once put it, "The unleashed power of the atom has changed everything save our modes of thinking, and thus we drift toward unparalleled catastrophe."[3] Unfortunately, too many of us—politicians, as well as the man in the street— still tend to talk about war as if it were the old-fashioned kind of dangerous but somewhat glamorous adventure—an expected though regrettable part of the pattern of human life. But the fantastic power of modern weapons of war requires that we cast our thinking in drastic new patterns. Man now has the undoubted power to destroy himself in not just one, but at least three entirely independent ways.

The first way is by *nuclear weapons.* The United States alone has enough fissionable material available to make a forty-million megaton bomb, several thousand times more powerful than is needed to wipe out all life on earth. The Federation of American Scientists supports this assertion with the terse statement: "With the stockpile . . . that now exists it is possible to cover the entire earth with radiation level which for ten years would remain sufficiently intense to prove fatal to all living beings on land."[4]

The second possible method of destruction is the use of *gas.* Without question, both we and the Russians have enough gas stockpiled to wipe out the human race.

The third road to race suicide is the use of *bacteriological weapons.* A little more than a glassful of one strain of botulinus toxin would suffice for the job if it could be properly distributed. Both of these last two methods have the ironic strategic advantage of leaving buildings and property undamaged, while destroying all life, making a sort of universal ghost town a real possibility.

---

[3]Albert Einstein, quoted on title page, Alice F. Bryant, *Radiation and the Race* (Philadelphia: American Friends Service Committee, April 10, 1959).

[4]Federation of American Scientists, statement of November 23, 1958.

Strangely enough, the very magnitude of destruction involved in the use of any one of these three methods, coupled with the constant and now almost casual reference to the possibility of their use, have combined to produce a certain apathetic indifference. Statistics concerning nuclear war are so prosaic that they are no longer worth repeating. Just after World War II and Hiroshima a favorite illustration for many speakers, guaranteed to have built-in shock value, was a reference to the cover of the *Bulletin of Atomic Scientists* with its dramatic clock face, the hands pointing to two minutes until midnight. Any experienced public speaker knows that today that kind of illustration has lost its ability to disturb.

Still, underneath this surface apathy, is there not in all of us an inner turmoil that will not be quieted, a creeping fear of utter extinction which has burrowed into the secret depths of our collective nature? I am not speaking of that fear of physical death which is a part of the psychological make-up of every normal human being. What I am referring to is an acid of dread which erodes the foundations of the entire community of men. It is an unstable pool of unfaced anxieties which constantly manifest themselves on the surface of existence, disguised in any number of ways. It is the fear of racial oblivion. For instance, the pace of living is abnormally accentuated. Men must get what they think they want quickly, for no one knows what tomorrow may bring, or whether there will be a tomorrow—for ourselves, for our neighbors, for our children, or for the race as a whole. Whether what we seek is material gain, physical pleasure, or long-desired economic, social, or political privileges, the goal must be achieved *now*. Patience and reason have little force against these frantic inner drives.

Another result of the pressure of this fear is our impatience with long, drawn-out, indecisive crises. We are tempted to fall victim to the dilemma of unrealistic alternatives and unanalyzed choices, best symbolized by a slogan which originated in Germany, "*Lieber rot als tot.*" That slogan has translated itself into not only the language, but also the attitudes, of people all over the world: "Better Red than dead!" To which men who pride themselves on patriotism angrily retort, "No! Better dead than Red!" Such slogans present our human predicament as allowing only two totally desperate alternatives, either universal atomic death or complete submission to Communist tyranny. For any man who is unwilling to surrender his moral reason in cowardly submission to technological or historical determinism, these two alternatives actually leave no room for choice. How can one choose intelligently between a world dominated by the Communists and one devastated by nuclear holocaust? Yet, a considerable public opinion in our country seems to think that we must end the Cold War by precipitating a hot one, or else give in to the Marxist tyranny.

In this kind of world, where does the Christian stand? He stands, if I properly understand the Gospel, in the most difficult of positions—the big middle. He stands there by virtue of the fact that, against the background of the New Testament and the moral demands of his faith in the living God, he cannot concede that "Red or dead" represent the only alternatives open to men. He stands in the big middle because he must maintain that, with a force so infinitely powerful as the love let loose in the world through Jesus Christ, even the unthinkable force of the thermonuclear bomb is ultimately challenged by its master. He stands in the big middle because he is certain that all the things nailed down are not loose, but that there are values, meanings, realities which still cannot be shaken, even in a world grown gray and horrible through the threat of atomic destruction.

What are these "unshakeable things?" One of which the Christian speaks with certainty is the nature of man. The insights of the Christian Gospel into the inner sanctum of man's personality carry with them the insistence that man's nature is a constant in human history, one of those rare things which is in effect "nailed down."

What is man? There is no simple answer to that question.

Writes the Psalmist, "Thou hast made him a little lower than the angels" (Psalm 8:5). Man is Adam in the Garden, Moses on the mountain, Noah drunken and naked in his tent, David with Bathsheba in the bedchamber, Isaiah in the Temple, Peter warming at the enemies' fire, Jesus of Nazareth on the Cross. Man is morally ambiguous, made in the image of God, but fashioned from the dust of the ground. Capable of the grossest evil, he can also by God's grace rise to sublime heights of moral achievement. The words of Alexander Pope are profound and descriptive:

> "Created half to rise and half to fall,
> Great Lord of all things, yet the prey of all,
> Sole judge of truth, in endless error hurled,
> The glory, jest, and riddle of the world."

No view of man which obscures the dark and twisted side of his nature is realistic. While it is a bitter pill for proud mankind to swallow, such a total view of man is essential, if we are to face with any creative hope the terror of the nuclear age. "Human nature," remarked Mark Twain, "is a commodity which seems to be widely distributed among the human race." That means, for one thing, that Dr. Paul Ramsay and other worthies to the contrary, there are no "un-do-able" dimensions of perversity. It may be unthinkable to conjure up the picture of a world covered with the dead rot of all humanity, but the reality behind that picture is by no means impossible. One may desire to class as "un-do-able" the pressing of a button which would irretrievably condemn humanity to oblivion, but one cannot review the history of man's concrete sin—the Nazi death camps, for instance—and rule *any* action out of the arsenal of human possibilities.

Too many of us live with the assumption—conscious or unconscious—that in the final analysis nuclear war is humanly impossible. Especially do we find it difficult to conceive of a destruction which would involve us, our families, and our immediate world. But our Christian faith unequivocably reminds us, "It can happen here!" It reminds us that man's nature is infected with a virus of evil whose limits are unpredictable. That "all have sinned" is not a verdict passed only on certain individual men, classes, groups, or nations. The confessional words of the Apostle Paul are the most universal of litanies: "That which I ought to do, I do not." One can hardly avoid the incisive judgment of a college sophomore, "You just have to admit that man is a primordial stinker." That judgment becomes more than a clever phrase when one reflects that man is a primordial stinker with a hydrogen bomb in his hand.

While these are true words, they do not complete, fortunately, the Christian understanding of man. Were this all that could be said, it might well be that the atomic mushroom cloud, that visible breath of the spirit of universal death, could be classed as a cruel blessing, wiping out evil as the gardener destroys pests with his spray.

Alongside the reality of human evil, however, is another truth, just as important, just as unshakeable. Our nineteenth-century forebears were admittedly overly optimistic and almost absurdly naive about human possibilities. The English historian, Isaac Taylor, could persuade himself, less than a hundred years ago, that "we are about to see the relics of barbarism, polygamy, infanticide, legalized prostitution, capricious avarice, sanguinary and immoral games, infliction of torture, slavery, and caste—disappear from the advancing world."[5]

One wonders how Professor Taylor might have reacted to Hiroshima, or the London blitz, or Buchenwald. In our day, such sentiments sound almost comical—in a heart-broken sort of way—but we must not forget that, from an opposite viewpoint, we can be equally blind and therefore cynical. Man *is* depraved in his every part, but every part of man *is not* totally depraved and sinful. High resolutions, noble purposes, sacrificial loves, valorous causes—such terms may ring hollowly in the harsh echo chambers of the disillusioned twentieth-century mind, but the words still possess power and reality. Christians must never forget that their faith insists not only upon the bankruptcy of human

[5]Isaac Taylor, *Ultimate Civilization*, quoted by Fishwick, *Ibid.*, p. 12.

sin, but also upon the endless resources of human redemption. Man's struggle with sin is never ending, but the Gospel proclaims that an unseen Ally of most formidable proportions is with us in the struggle.

Unless we believe that God has capitulated to the forces of evil and abandoned His creation to the powers of destruction, Christian believers are never entitled to throw in the towel in the struggle for peace. With eyes wide open to the perversities of every human endeavor, yet with heart and mind wide open to the grace of God, the Christian asserts that nuclear war and destruction, burned out cities, deformed and mutilated posterity, contaminated earth, and polluted atmosphere are not the final and inevitable summary of existence. These things are not the will of God. Since every disciple is committed by his faith to the prayer, "Thy will be done in earth as it is in heaven," he is also committed to the assurance that a relative peace among nations is a live option for mankind.

If man were only a beast, without eternal horizons, then we might accept war and destruction as the normal and continuing characteristics of human life, for such is the lot of the beast. But man is not just an animal; he is created in the divine image. True, he has rebelled against the lordship of his Creator, but there remains within him, by the grace of God, the possibility of redemption. To each man, God has given mind and passions. Both easily become the handmaidens of evil, but redeemed minds and passions may become instruments for God's purposes of peace.

Every redeemed man must realize, however, that he functions in the midst of a largely unredeemed world. Such a context severely limits the alternatives for creative action by the servants of God. No possibility exists for a perfect pattern of performance, either for men or nations. Christians should be most acutely aware of their own failures and imperfections. They ought to know that no Christian pathway to peace, in the sense of some course of action which is both totally right and completely successful, actually exists. No one can contend, for instance, that the United Nations is a total answer to the world's hunger for peace.

Rather, it is one of many structures which represent man's valid striving for peace and world order. Disarmament talks, nuclear test bans, regional peace-keeping organizations, common markets —no one of these is *the* answer, certainly not *the Christian* answer. But the simple fact is that *the* answer has not presented itself among the available alternatives. Therefore, thinking Christian men face the necessity of involving themselves in a complex and continuing struggle for peace. The methods used may often be morally questionable; the achievable end is always a relative, never an absolute, accomplishment. But, by virtue of his faith, the Christian man is inescapably involved, for whatever creative possibilities lie within the mind and heart of redeemed man must be cast into the balance on the side of peace.

Let me suggest one other unshakeable insight of the Gospel of Jesus Christ. Men—not just man in the abstract but individual human beings—are loved of God. True, this love is unmerited and totally of grace, but the simple fact of being loved by God confers upon men an infinite value in the eyes of any other child of God. Each Christian finds himself in a continuing paradox at this point. Like the Apostle Paul, he looks at himself honestly before God and cries out, "I am the chief of sinners." But also like Paul, he turns his gaze from himself to others, and, seeing his brother men invested with infinite value by the love of God he cries out, "Would that I were accursed, that my brethren might be saved!"

As a result of this recognition of the worth of all men through grace, we must involve ourselves in the struggle for something which drastically affects the life of all men: peace among nations. "The love of Christ constrains us"—not only his love for me, which I cannot explain and do not merit, but his love for my brother, whom I also, by his grace, must love. Against this background, I cannot accept the glib declaration of the supernationalist, "My country, right or wrong!" I must reject his heated assertion that if we only insure the continued existence of a non-personal entity called the United States (an entity which is assumed, strangely enough, to go on existing even after its nearly 200 million citizens have been transformed into nearly 200 megacorpses), it does not then matter what happens to the other millions of human beings on this planet. As an American, I am rightfully concerned about the life and welfare of my fellow Americans. But as a Christian, I am also concerned about the welfare of every human being everywhere.

That nuclear warfare allows no easy moral answers for the Christian ought to be obvious, but it is almost ludicrous to see the warped perversities in which even Christians become involved in an attempt to devise such easy, black-and-white answers. Listen to Lieutenant General William K. Harrison in an article in *Christianity Today* called "A Christian General's View: Is Nuclear War Justifiable?"[6] General Harrison's answer to his question is, given the circumstances of enemy aggression and attack, an unqualified "Yes." Not only does he reach this conclusion, which he certainly has a right to believe, but he goes further and contrives to make wholesale nuclear destruction a prop for the moral purposes of God. He writes, "Since the bombings of World War II, and now nuclear weapons, the entire aggressor nation, guilty as it is, no longer is shielded by armies and navies. It, the real force, the real will behind the military weapons, can be attacked directly instead of only after the defeat of its military forces. By supporting the ambitions of its ruler, it shares his guilt and accepts the same risks as do the military forces themselves. Therefore, such loss as it does sustain can be laid to its own aggression, not to its innocence."[7]

The bland conclusion which General Harrison reaches is infinitely shocking in its implications. If we are attacked by another nation, he tells us, we are then morally justified in assuming that we have been appointed instruments of God to bring judgment in nuclear form upon every citizen—man, woman, child—in that enemy land, to wipe them off the face of the earth. Such a view appears to me to be the height of self-righteous de-

[6]William K. Harrison, "A Christian General's View: Is Nuclear War Justifiable?," *Christianity Today*, VII, No. 19 (June 21, 1963), p. 913.

[7]*Ibid.*, p. 913.

lusion and the epitome of man's ability to rationalize his own weakness and sin. It is significant that General Harrison continually refers to the enemy nation as "it." It is easier to think about raining atomic bombs on "it" than on "them," the millions of human beings, basically like ourselves, who make up any nation.

Given the simple statement of John 3:16, "For God so loved the world that he gave his only begotten son . . .," this one thing ought to be clear and precise in enlightened Christian thinking: the wholesale and indiscriminate slaughter of the inhabitants of cities, nations, continents, or civilizations can never be blithely identified as "the will of God." If such actions come, if such a holocaust develops, it will be the result not only of the sins of other nations but of our own. The guilt will be ours as well as that of the Russians or the Chinese. The core of our guilt may well lie in the fact that we have striven far harder to prepare for wars than to establish peace; that we have gagged at the "gnat" of investing millions in the United Nations while swallowing the "camel" of billions invested in the race to the moon; that we have been far more willing to run the certain risk of atomic testing than the uncertain risk of nuclear test bans; that we have allowed abstractions, dogmas, systems, and slogans to outweigh the value of human personality; and that, too often, we Christians have left whatever serious attempts are being made for peace largely to noble and sincere pagans who have no real knowledge of God's redeeming love.

This brings us to the final thing that is nailed down in our chaotic world. In all our struggle, our despair, our frustration, we cannot afford to lose sight of the powerful grace of God. The Christian makes his eternal confession, "This is my Father's world." God is still on His throne, He is not dead, and His arm is still powerful to save. In God's world the struggle for peace is infinitely important. Faced with the incredible horror of nuclear war, we have no choice but to seek for constantly new and productive alternatives in the fight for peace. The disillusioned cynic who holds that only physical existence has any meaning may argue, "Better Red than dead." The jingoistic rabble-rouser, playing to the galleries, may shout, "Better dead than Red!" But the concerned Christian, always in the middle, must go on painfully, sacrificially, earnestly seeking the will of God which means neither Red nor dead.

Life in the Christian middle is never easy. The road to peace and freedom is among the most strenuous and sacrificial of journeys. The process can never be quick; there are no instant recipes for peace. To the disappointment of most partisan politicians, there is no one thing the President, the State Department, or Congress can do which will insure peace. As we should have learned by now, a change of parties in power does not solve the world crisis. Despite our American pretensions, there are some things which happen all the time on this troubled globe that cannot be altered by *anything* our President does or does not do. We Christians must recognize these hard truths and learn to live with them. We must adjust ourselves to a long struggle for peace which can neither be painless nor easy. Indeed, that struggle may well involve one of the most painful of all experiences: shedding, as individuals and as a nation, some cherished but ill-founded assumptions and precious prejudices about our own power, our own national righteousness, and our own lack of responsibility for world order. We must give ourselves to a difficult, nerve-wracking, frustratingly long struggle if we are to serve both peace and freedom.

As Christians, how can any one of us doubt, despite the dangers and the problems, that the struggle will be worth it all? How can we justify turning our backs? Unashamedly, as one Christian, I confess that I want my children to live, and my grandchildren to be born, normal and whole, in a world that will sustain existence and offer the opportunity for creative living. I want my loved ones to grow up enjoying both peace and freedom. But I cannot give these things to my children, if all I can offer my country is a pep rally admonition, "Go get 'em, Uncle Sam!" The building of such a world will require painstaking struggle and peace within order. It will also demand that I, along with more and more men everywhere, come to understand that which has been clearly revealed to the followers of Jesus Christ—that, in the grace of God, all men are bound up in the same bundle. We are constantly asked today, "Can we coexist with the Communist evil?" I can only answer that we are coexisting with it, and furthermore, that the Christian community has been coexisting with evil and sin of one kind or another for 2000 years. This does not mean we accept that evil, or cease to fight it. Our deepest convictions impel us to struggle against it in every possible or practical way. Our unchanging goal is not only a world of peace, but a world in which every man is free to be a man. But let us be brutally clear. The chances are overwhelmingly strong that if nuclear war comes, there will be no free men anywhere. Even if there should be survivors, there would be no chance, in a devastated earth, of any real freedom. There is a sense in which the question of coexistence was answered at Hiroshima. With the dropping of the first atomic bomb, we entered an age in which, like it or not, the whole human race is literally going to live or die together.

5.

THE THINGS THAT AFFECT PEACE

Charles Wells
Editor and Publisher, Between the Lines
Princeton, New Jersey

What are the things that affect peace? First, consider threats to peace in our time.

The first threat to peace is *Communism.* I do not belittle it at all.

The second threat is *us.*

The Communists would like to conquer the world and we who are too lazy or too hysterical to keep up with it as we should, know little about this political cancer. Communism is the first threat to peace because Communists still intend to conquer the world. Because I emphasize how Communism is weakening and changing does not mean that I am "soft on Communism." If Communists were not in existence today we would still have very serious problems to threaten peace. We would have Nasser, we would have all of Africa and its tumult, we would have Castro. Castro would have very much the same philosophy he now has: to destroy the rich, to take the wealth away from the few and give it to the many, and in the meantime, to make himself the political master of this hemisphere. The philosophy of Nazism, the philosophy of Mussolini, and the philosophy of Franco parallel the philosophy of Communism. There is that combination of personal opportunism and personal ambition plus the spirit of Anti-Christ. In some real sense, the Anti-Christ is here. This evil spirit is in all those who offer people a way of being saved from their illiteracy, their diseases, and their despair in terms of political opportunism and personal political ambition. The spirit of the Anti-Christ has been in men like Hitler, Mussolini, Franco, Castro, and Batista before him, as they offered a false way of hope and salvation.

Communism is the Anti-Christ of our day and the first threat to the peace of our people and the peace of the world. I can document this in the words of Nikita Khrushchev. In 1960, when Khrushchev was in this country, in Los Angeles, those who interviewed him had joked with him a great deal about his going to church on Sunday. He was in America, they pointed out, and to understand America he should go to church. It angered him a little bit. Harrison Salisbury, one of the newsmen with him who spoke fluent Russian, made this point and it stung Khrushchev a little. An hour later in an interview Khrushchev got excited and said, "Let me tell you about Communism. We know war, we intend to conquer the world all right, but how? You folks go to church, but we are doing what Jesus taught."

That was blasphemy. Communists who say that they do as Jesus taught, helping people, reveal that they themselves are conscious, in a way, that they speak for the Anti-Christ. If you read *Das Kapital* and the *Communist Manifesto,* then read Lenin's long volume on Marxism, and Stalin's brief essays on Leninism, you will find that war is merely one of the avenues of conquest. Communists will utilize every national war, or war of liberation, to advance their cause if they can. But war is only one of the avenues of attack. In fact, war is only one of the minor instruments of their revolution. You would have to hunt a long time to find any paragraph in which the Communists ever wrote, "We'll win by war," although there are rare paragraphs which do say this. There is such a statement in Lenin's third volume describing imperialism, written before World War I. At that time the white man stood in all his pride over all of Asia and

Africa. Lenin said that as the colonial peoples fight to free themselves from international imperial powers, they will wage a great conflict. He said that in that great conflict the Communist Party would throw all of itself into the great international struggle out of which would emerge chaos, and that only the Marxists will have the skill and the plans to bring order out of this chaos.

The Marxists do not teach that they will conquer the world by the force of Russian military power. Their plan is always to utilize the conflicts that come. They teach that they will promote revolution by violence. Was it a Russian army that conquered China for Communism? No. It was a Chinese revolutionary army made up of the masses of peasants and workers. Was it the Russian army that invaded South Korea to take it over? No. It was the North Korean Communist Army.

Name the place where there is danger from Communism and you will find a nation that is politically corrupt, industrially or economically backward, with the people hungry and desperate. The Marxists teach that it is the task of the international Communist Party to infiltrate that area, to organize a native army, and to arm it and train it so that the revolution may come from within, as in Cuba. Therefore, the Russians go in as technicians, they go in with weapons. This, however, is not quite the same thing as war. Since war has become a profit-making business, we have failed to analyze the most dangerous point, that the Reds will infiltrate any area where revolution is ready. They will infiltrate, agitate, and promote the revolution from within. They teach that the world will be won to Communism, not through a Russian invasion, but through infiltration, agitation, Marxist subversion, and violent internal revolution.

The Russians have a word for agitation for which we have no equivalent. The old Russian peasant home was made of logs, and there is a key log, a long log in the center of the floor that sticks out at the end. When they take a house down, they do it very quickly and save the logs. They don't take the logs down one by one, off the top. They hitch an ox, or a tractor these days, to the end of this key log and jerk back and forth. Then the whole thing falls apart. That word that the Russians use to describe shaking the key log is also the word they use for agitation. It means to shake to pieces from underneath. So remember the order: first there is Marxist infiltration, Marxist education, internal agitation, and then revolution from within. The Russians finance the revolution, send in technicians and equipment; but the army must be indigenous. Because this system works, they have used it in Iran. They have used it in Indonesia. They have used it in Vietnam. There United States soldiers are fighting the natives of Vietnam who have become Communists. They are not fighting the Russians. You see how clever this is. Communism is dangerous precisely because it is so clever. It makes us fight little people everywhere, but not the Russians. They have forced us to do a terrible thing, to kill little people in order to stop Communism.

I do not consider Communism a small danger. It is a great danger. It is a much greater danger than we realize, because the weapons we have built are totally inadequate. In the last ten years we have spent at least 100 billion dollars on weapons to stop Communism. Yet nobody can find anything to stop Communism in Cuba. We could blow Cuba off the map in twenty seconds, kill every Cuban, and leave the land desolate. What would that do to stop Communism? It would only convince all Latin America that we are their enemy; and those little people who are hungry, who want a change in their way of life, would fear we would kill them, too. We have spent 100 billion dollars on bombs and missiles and yet we can't do anything about Communism in Cuba except perhaps to kill Cubans.

Lenin even taught that one of the great mistakes in promoting Communism would be to start a revolution before it is ripe. He urged his followers never to spring the revolution until they were sure that the government they were infiltrating was so corrupt and the people so desperately poor that they would die before they would accept another month of it. Communists wait until the revolution of the proletariat is so well-organized that it will not fail. They do not start the revolution until they are certain that the proletariat can take over and prevent outside capitalistic powers from coming in. Communists strive to prevent the capitalist powers from getting involved in a great war of total destruction, leaving little for a new Communist state to work with.

Communism is a major threat to peace.

Next to stating that Communism is a threat to peace, however, it must be said that Americans, too, are a threat to peace. By our ignorance, our hysteria, and our seduction by the profits from armaments, we are a threat to peace. At the present time we blush for shame that many of our congressmen are practically under orders not to let any defense contracts get cancelled in their area. Congressmen get re-elected if they can keep those contracts rolling in. Our own blind drive for bigger armaments has carried us to the point that we have become, next to Communism, the greatest threat to peace.

There is an organization called the Air Force Association, made up of multi-million dollar corporations that make planes and missiles. Many of their executives are retired from the high command of the Air Force. I have attended the Air Force Association meetings. There is a lot of drinking and a lot of wild talking about the great threat of Communism. In that atmosphere, we were told for several years of the bomber gap, and we kept on making B-36's, B-47's, and B-52's. The B-36's are still sitting all over the world. Pilots have never wanted to fly them because not many flyers wanted to trust their lives in them. They never were much good, but we kept making them. Finally it was found out that there was no bomber gap. We had spent six billion dollars on bombers and the development of them until we had nearly 1500 of them. And at last it was learned that Russia never had more than 160 long-range bombers. We built 1500, and most of the Russian bombers could not cross the ocean and return. That news never got out, however, until the money had been spent. Now you can meet many an Air Force officer who will grin and admit, "Yeah, that was something, wasn't it? They never had over 150."

A great deal has also been said of the missile gap. In recent years there has been a big push for missiles. Whichever party was out of power made the country's defense a hot political issue—bomber gap, missile gap, credibility gap and so forth. Truman said there was no bomber gap. Eisenhower said there was no missile gap. Now it is common knowledge that there has never been a missile gap. We probably have from 900 to 1000 missiles packed and ready to shoot, including Polaris missiles. No one knows the exact total because this is all classified information. In comparison to our 900 to 1000 missiles, the Russians are estimated to have less than 250 missiles ready. We have four times their missile strength. This has been widely known among scientists, and can easily be documented. We have 40,000 megatons of plutonium ready. This is 40,000 megatons of nuclear explosive, and Russia has about 8,000. We are five times as heavily armed as they are. We could destroy Russia over and over again. But they could also destroy us over and over again. The question now is, how dead can you get?

Now you can see why I say that we are the second danger to peace. Ralph E. Lapp, one of the top nuclear physicists, in his book, *Kill and Overkill,* discusses many of these things. He says that we are so much more heavily armed than Russia that we are keeping them fearful. You have no idea how scared they are. Ralph Lapp gave a classified bit of information that the Pentagon has neither denied nor affirmed about a B-52 that had an accident over the Carolinas. The B-52 was on a military practice run in which a hydrogen bomb accidentally fell. You have been told how we're protected, how it is impossible for an accident to take place. You have been told that there are six triggers which must be sprung. Ralph Lapp reported that of the six triggers that have to be sprung, when that bomb was found, five of the six had already gone off. There was just one left. That was a massive hydrogen bomb. Most of the Carolinas would have been destroyed. If that plane had been wiped out by its own bomb and half the Carolinas destroyed, do you think the military whose job is to hit quick would have called Moscow and asked, "Was that one of yours?" These military men operate on the thesis that whoever hits first will win the war. Strategic Air Command's business is, the minute there is any sign of attack, to hit Russia with everything, because he who hits first gets the advantage.

After this brief look at the two great major threats to peace, consider now some of the things that make for peace.

The first step toward peace is a disciplined world. We will have an undisciplined world as long as we have extremist movements. If there were no such thing as Communism, there would still be all kinds of extremists and opportunists. There would still be the hunger and the exploitation and the fear of the common people around the world. Men like Franco of Spain, not a Communist, are also tyrants. There is actually more freedom for evangelicals in Moscow than in Madrid. An undisciplined society will always produce either its Communists, its Fascists, or its other extremists. This is what makes peace almost impossible. There simply can be no peace in an undisciplined society.

Now what is the nature of the discipline we need? The first-century Christian would say that the only discipline would be the discipline of love.

Most of the world is non-Christian. The main concern in this context is not to talk about how to make Christians of them, but to consider how to keep the world from being destroyed in thirty minutes. The United States and Russia can destroy themselves. In that holocaust Canada and the northern part of Latin America would also be destroyed; and whatever destroys Russia will terribly decimate Europe, and multiplied millions will die. Arthur Hadley, author of *National Security and Arms Control,* interviewed the leading physicists in the world today, the men who created the atomic age. These men share the conviction that from 90 to 140 million Americans will die, and from 100 million to 170 million Russians will die in case of a nuclear war. Tens of millions more would die from radiation poison that would take months to be felt and identified. We have reached the place where an undisciplined world with unbridled, fanatical power groups means self-destruction.

Can there be discipline with extremists, with fanatical opportunists who are competing with each other for power? Franco thought that he was the champion of the Mediterranean, and maybe more. Hitler had power lines over the world. Castro is openly promoting revolutions throughout Latin America. Nasser, moving towards an atomic arsenal, considers himself the father of nationalism for colonial Africa. Is there any hope for peace in that sort of picture?

Is nationalism the answer? One way to see this is in our own history as a people. In earlier times every man carried a weapon, and every man was a law unto himself. When a crime was committed, it was often too far to get the marshal in another county. Therefore, the law was taken into the hands of the man who had the gun. As civilization progressed in the West, the time finally came when each good citizen who was prepared to defend his home with his own gun, saw that anarchy was growing. Finally, therefore, it was agreed by the people as a whole that the federal marshal and the sheriff and the police should be the only ones to carry guns. The citizen submitted his power to the administration of higher authorities. There had to be some surrender of sovereignty.

There was a time when the states of New York and Pennsylvania stood at the brink of war, but the time came when they had to surrender their right to make war to the national sovereignty of these United States of America.

We are at the point now when, obviously, everybody will not check in his atom bombs and missiles. The first step would be to quit making them. This is a little step. If we are to have a disciplined world, we must take the atomic six-shooters out of the hands of the fanatics and get them into the hands of the superior forces called humanity.

To show further where we are and why we must stop multiplying destructive weapons, consider some of the findings of a commission of engineers and scholars, headed by Seymour Melman, professor of industrial engineering at Columbia University. Dr. Benjamin Spock, the famous child specialist, also participated. This report presents evidence that we are overbuilding our weapons by several hundred percent. The thousands of missiles and bombers we now have could destroy every city in the Soviet Union with a population of 100,000 or more a thousand times! The Russians can destroy us about 100 times over. It only takes one or two megatons to destroy any big city—at the most three megatons. We have 40,000 megatons. There are not more than twenty-five or thirty cities in Russia of 100,000 or more people. This is why the top scientists are all saying that we must stop the arms race, getting the means of world destruction out of the hands of undisciplined societies and into the hands of a disciplined world. There are only two ways to do that—first, quit making arms, and then, get them under control.

Then the next step towards peace is some international authority that represents justice, law, and obedience to law for all people. I am not going to discuss the United Nations. I will only say that if you kill the United Nations on Saturday, you'll have to start something just like it on Monday or live in ultimate chaos. We cannot live in a world that is this crowded and in which men can destroy themselves in thirty minutes, without having something in the way of over-all discipline. The United Nations, or something that grows out of it, is the best political hope for a disciplined society.

To repeat, we must stop making atomic weapons, and then get the ones now existing under some rational control whereby it is agreed that they shall never be used except under certain circumstances. Then, after another generation has passed, such an international authority can be established that will put nuclear weapons out of business completely. We would only have those weapons which are necessary for police authority. The alternative to such a plan is World War III.

So these are the things that make for peace, practical steps we must take. In my opinion, there is no other way.

6.

THE UNITED NATIONS, AN INSTRUMENT OF PEACE

CHARLES WELLBORN
Chaplain
Florida State University
Tallahassee, Florida

A delegate to a recent denominational meeting offered a resolution from the floor concerning the United Nations. The motion, if passed, would have directed all agencies of the denomination, in all their published literature, to designate the United Nations Organization not only as an "instrument of peace," but also as an "instrument of war." Such a resolution carries many marks of a current, widespread type of muddy thinking and biased prejudice. Sir Leslie Monro, long New Zealand's chief representative at the UN, has written, "Ignorance of the aims and authority of the United Nations ranges from those who regard it as a world legislature to those who dismiss it as a futile or dangerous debating society."[1]

Even though the motion referred to was not adopted, let me hasten to comply with it—at least, literally. The United Nations is an "instrument of peace," though it is not the Utopian cure-all which some people believe it is. But, shaped by the realism of a world of strife and division, the United Nations is also called upon, in pursuit of peace, to act (in Katanga or the Gaza Strip,

[1]Sir Leslie Monro, *United Nations: Hope for a Divided World* (New York: Holt, 1960), p. 8.

for instance) as an "instrument of war," functioning through force and violence. The fact is, if the UN were not sometimes prepared to act as an "instrument of war," it could never become an "instrument of peace."

All of this points up the central question: What is the United Nations? A clear, factual understanding of the answer to that question would make unnecessary any serious consideration of the resolution. Such an answer is needed by many Americans and, especially, by American Christians. Precise understanding would relieve the United Nations, on the one hand, of the inflated expectations of its more enthusiastic supporters and, on the other hand, of the bitter indictments of its most vehement critics.

On July 28, 1945, by a vote of 89 to 2, the American Senate ratified the United Nations Charter, signed in San Francisco a month before. Three days earlier than the Senate action, a Gallup Poll reported that 66 per cent of the American people were favorable to the United Nations, 31 per cent undecided and only 3 per cent definitely opposed.

Clearly, the overwhelming majority of Americans supported the United Nations at the time of its formation. What did they expect from it? Some, to be sure, were overly optimistic. President Wilson's League of Nations had failed, they felt, largely because the United States was not a part of it. Now a new international organization had been established, this time including all the world's major powers. Surely, this meant success. The United Nations was "mankind's best hope for peace, a new gateway to a world of harmony and co-operation."

But this was not the whole story. A healthy dose of realism prevented most Americans, even at the beginning, from expecting too much. Those who attack the United Nations today because, so they say, it has failed to keep the peace, need to be reminded that, according to a Gallup Poll of July 25, 1945 (two weeks before American ratification of the charter), only 15 per cent of all Americans questioned thought that the United Nations could prevent all wars. Fifty-four per cent of them felt that the United

States would have to fight another major war within fifty years. These figures indicate that a surprising number of Americans realistically linked their hopes for peace with some understanding of the true status, aims, and limitations of the United Nations.

If most people were neither naive nor Utopian in their view of the UN, what fundamental motive led them to support it? The simplest answer is "peace," but peace is an abstract concept which must be solidified to be useful. Of course most men want peace, but the lesson of history is that the "peace" of a sinful society is maintained only through power, structure, and organization. It does not establish itself. The peace of the Roman Empire, or that of the *Pax Britannica* in the nineteenth century, was dependent on a pattern of power, molded into a functioning "instrument" for peace.

What type of structure can most effectively help to maintain peace? In the absence of world dictatorship, or of the overpowering and unquestioned superiority of one nation over all others, international order can come only through some concert of the nations. Such international co-operation must assume concrete form. The form may have many variations. One tragic error in the League of Nations was that it was set up primarily to maintain the *status quo*. Such a system emphasized order with little regard for the demands of justice. All change was, almost by definition, undesirable. The United Nations charter, on the other hand, represents an attempt to meet the requirements of both order and justice. Its basic concept is that of collective security, but the kind of collective security envisioned is, in the words of Ernest Gross, ". . . a system which assures that illicit ends cannot be achieved by any means, whereas legitimate ends can be achieved by proper means."[2] Thus, the ideal purpose of the United Nations may be set out as the achievement of an international structure for the maintenance of peace, flexible enough to move toward enforcement of order and also to provide workable means for peaceable change in the relationships among nations.

---

[2]Ernest Gross, *The United Nations* (New York: Harper, 1962).

In our kind of world—one which has made little progress beyond the concept of the nation-state as the ultimate center of political loyalty and power—any international structure must necessarily be primitive. Even a primitive organization, however, if it is to be at all effective, requires three basic elements:

(1) A broad consensus of agreement as to the principles which govern both ends and means in international relationships;

(2) Machinery for applying the principles to specific situations;

(3) A general will to use the machinery.

The United Nations Charter provides a broad framework of principles. It offers also a network of international machinery. The structure could be of great effectiveness in maintaining peace, but whether the machinery is actually used, and whether the principles set out in the Charter actually constitute a consensus for action, depend almost entirely on the third factor: the will of states to use the United Nations as an instrument for peace. Consequently, the actual capabilities of the UN are determined, not by theory or supposition, but by trial and error. Its so-called "failures" are, in almost every case, not dependent on defects in its own organization but on the difficulties experienced by member nations in reaching agreement.

What this means must be squarely faced by both the friends and foes of the United Nations. The UN is not a substitute for power politics but a part of the complex world pattern of such politics. A nation, however well-intentioned, cannot delegate its responsibilities in any area of foreign policy to the United Nations and, so to speak, "let the UN take care of it." The United Nations is a political mechanism through which national policy is constantly expressed by each member nation. It is a technical instrument, which may or may not be successful or even usable in specific cases. Moreover, it is a fluid structure always evolving and adapting itself to the situations in which its resources are applied. It is, above all, totally responsive to the general will of its nation-members.

Is the United Nations worthy of the interest and support of

American Christians? The answer to this query cannot be given in any abstract or generalized manner, much less by repeating slogans. Though ill-informed people tend to believe otherwise, the United Nations is in itself neither angelic nor demonic. Those who make vague, emotional appeals for all-out, non-discriminating support of the United Nations tend to claim for it far more than it is capable of accomplishing, at least in its present form. On the other hand, a vocal minority in the United States assails the UN as a devilish superstate, or as a subversive instrumentality of world Communism. It is interesting that those who attack the United Nations as a superstate, encroaching dangerously on American sovereignty, are apt also to criticize the organization most severely at the precise times when it most clearly reveals its basic incapacity to act as a superstate, as in the Hungarian crisis of 1956. That crisis emphasized the fact that the United Nations is finally dependent on the will of its member-states and the hard facts of national power distribution in the world. A fully developed system of political order punishes all acts which the system defines as crimes, but the UN can treat as crimes only those acts which the nations themselves are willing and prepared to punish. In the Hungarian situation, while the collective moral judgment of the world condemned the Russian actions, most nations, including the United States, were not willing to risk involvement in a nuclear world conflict in order to punish the crime. As a result, the United Nations was powerless to intervene.

The simple "ABCs" of world peace include these principles:

(1) There can be no lasting peace without a workable system of world order which provides for the solution of conflicts and problems by means other than international warfare;

(2) There can be no workable system of world order without enforceable world law;

(3) There can be no enforceable world law until the nations conceive it to be in their best interest to delegate to a world political structure the power to enforce law; and

(4) The United Nations cannot now function as such a system and gives no promise of doing so in the immediate future.

Only when enough members of the UN throw sufficient power behind its actions, as in the Congo crisis, can the world organization act as a true means of enforcing peace.

It is true that in the Congo the United Nations functioned as an "instrument of war"—just as the police force in our home town, though designed as an ultimate force for peace and order, must act with power or even violence in times of disturbance. But the UN could do this because a preponderance of the world's national powers supported its actions and approved them, while other powerful nations, who did not approve, did not count the situation important enough to their own national interest to oppose forcibly the United Nations' police actions.

What all of this indicates is that an intelligent American Christian needs to take a long hard look at the United Nations in terms of actual facts—not fiction—about its operation. Is the United Nations making a genuine contribution to the cause of world peace and order? Is it a threat to the objectives of American foreign policy and the safety of our own nation?

Let us consider the second of these questions first. What about the UN and American national interest? This is a legitimate question, since no nation can be expected to cooperate fully with anything which cuts across its own long-term interests. Some people have strong opinions on this matter. A recent letter to one of our denominational papers cancelled a subscription on the basis that the editor has allowed favorable remarks about the United Nations to appear and was, *ipso facto,* "playing into the hands of the Communist conspiracy." To be sure, the significance of this kind of viewpoint is not to be exaggerated, since a recent Gallup Poll shows that more than 85 per cent of the American people still feel that the United States should be a part of the United Nations. But the vocal, highly active opposition at least fulfills the function of requiring us all to take a closer look at the facts.

One approach which sheds light on the situation is to arrive at an American "batting average" in the UN. Here are some figures compiled by the World Rule of Law Center at Duke

University. Through the first sixteen years of UN operation sixty-two resolutions with significant content were voted on either by the Security Council or by the General Assembly. Four times, the United States abstained from voting. In the remaining fifty-eight decisions, the United States voted on the winning side fifty-five times. It was on the losing side only three times, and no one of those three votes involved any vital change in United States policy. Furthermore, the official report on the seventeenth General Assembly, presented to the Senate Committee on Foreign Relations by Senator Gore of Tennessee, a Democrat, and Senator Allot of Colorado, a Republican, stated: "The United States maintained its record of never having lost a UN vote of vital importance to its security interests."

The UN record can also be studied from another angle. It is important to realize that the Soviet Union has never won on a major resolution which it introduced and which the United States opposed. On the contrary, the record shows a continuing series of rebuffs, defeats, and condemnations aimed at Russia. Just from these two recent sessions, here is a partial list of such actions—a list which naturally does not include such earlier and more dramatic anti-Communist actions as the United Nations' intervention in Korea:

(1) The resolution of October, 1961, against the 50-megaton bomb;

(2) The December, 1961, resolution against practices depriving the people of Tibet of their rights and freedoms;

(3) The Hungary resolution of December, 1962, against the Soviet Union's continued disregard of UN resolutions and objectives;

(4) The September, 1960, resolution, rejecting the Soviet Union's attack on Secretary General Dag Hammerskjold and strengthening his hand in the Congo;

(5) The Cuba resolution of February 15, 1962, overwhelmingly rejecting a resolution calling on the United States to end its alleged interference in the internal affairs of Cuba;

(6) The December, 1962, resolution accepting the Advisory

Opinion of the International Court holding that costs of the Congo and Middle East operations are "expenses of the Organization," binding on members, a resolution bitterly opposed by the Soviet Union;

(7) The rejection of the seating of Communist China in the General Assembly; and

(8) The overwhelming rejection of the Soviet demand for a three-man committee or "troika" in place of the Secretary-General—without so much as a single non-Communist country supporting the Soviet position.

Actually, this list could go on almost indefinitely. On the basis of this kind of record, it is difficult—if not impossible—to argue that the United Nations' actions, up to this point, constitute any threat to the national self-interest of the United States. It is to be remembered also that our country possesses exactly the same veto power in the Security Council as does Russia, and though the Soviets have found it necessary to use that veto consistently, the United States has not done so at all. In addition, from a realistic viewpoint, the United States possesses at least an equal hard-power factor to that possessed by the Soviet Union. When the General Assembly condemned Russian interference in Hungary, such a resolution could probably have been effective only at the price of war. Any action involving a condemnation of any American policy would fall into the same category, unless our government was willing freely to consent to the UN action.

This kind of self-centered analysis of the United Nations is legitimate and valuable, but it is hardly sufficient for the Christian citizen. What about the long range objectives of those who are constrained by a universal Gospel to look beyond the narrow limits of national boundaries? What about the peace and well-being, not just of Americans, but of the whole world? Does the United Nations help in any way to bring us all closer to a society of at least relative peace and order? On the other side of the coin, since we know what kind of world the Communists appear to want, is the United Nations helping or hindering them in bringing about their kind of world order?

Once again, I think we must be reminded that the United Nations cannot be judged in Utopian or unrealistic terms. It is not a superstate; it is not even a federal union of nation-states. It possesses no real sovereignty. Moreover, it is not a confederation of democratic states, dedicated to the total achievement of Western ambitions. It is a loose conglomeration including states which, in many ways, appear to be mortal enemies to one another, but if the United Nations is to remain a *world* organization, rather than just another of many political alliances, with the opportunity to bring about any measure of reconciliation, it must continue to include both sides of the Cold War.

The United Nations must be rated, therefore, in terms of its actual performance under these circumstances. Judged without illusions, the organization does not come off badly at all. It does provide a forum for the expression of the world's collective moral conscience, and there is evidence that this conscience has added measurable weight to the recommendations and the mediating influence of the UN. It does provide contact and encounter between opposing world powers, with the resultant possibility, though never the guarantee, of some approach to settlement of controversy by peaceful means. On the secondary level of international relationships, in such areas as food distribution, aid to children, trade, literacy, and scientific cooperation, the UN has achieved notable success. In terms of specific action, the United Nations has many times proved its value in the building of a better world.

Look, for instance, at one of its most advanced and controversial actions. There is room for thoughtful criticism of some phases of the UN action in the Congo, but the over-all effect of that endeavor is now quite clear. In all the discussion of Katanga and Tshombe, some of us appear to have forgotten that, at its outset, the explosive Congolese situation offered the Communists their best opportunity in all of Africa for a Russian-backed showdown of black men against so-called white European imperialism. If there had been no UN, it is difficult to see how this triumph of

Communist strategy could have been avoided, short of a perilous, muzzle-to-muzzle encounter of major Cold War opponents.

When chaos broke out in the Congo following independence, the Congolese government appealed to both the United States and the Soviet Union for help. The Russians seized their opportunity and placed a hundred Russian trucks and ten Russian planes, with personnel, at the disposal of Patrice Lumumba. The United States wisely preferred to work through the United Nations. The Congolese government then invited the UN to send military assistance, and the rest of the story is well known. The Russians found it necessary to withdraw; a Cold War confrontation which might easily have become a "hot war" was avoided. Is it surprising that the Communists opposed the Congo action at every turn and still refuse to pay any part of its expenses? The incident represented a major defeat for Communist strategy in Africa.

Those who hold that the United Nations is an instrument for the Communist conspiracy are hard put to make a case with the facts. In the words of Arthur Larson, "They tell us that the Communists are really not against the United Nations, but only pretend to be, so as to trick all the rest of us into being for it. Presumably, the Soviet Union also laboriously maneuvers to get itself outvoted on such things as the United Nations' action in Korea, and all the other beatings it has taken at the hands of the UN. Why the Soviet Union wants to trick us all into supporting an organization which consistently clobbers Russia is not explained."[3]

Beyond this, however, is one supreme point which must be considered in shaping our attitude toward the United Nations. I refer to the crucial interest of Americans and of the whole human race in peace—an interest which demands that all practical steps be taken to avoid the holocaust of thermonuclear war. An enlightened Christian conscience must certainly impel us in this same direction. Anyone who tries, intelligently and responsibly,

---

[3]Arthur Larson, "What Every UN Critic Should Know" (*Saturday Review*, June 15, 1963), pp. 13-15.

to consider international affairs will not long remain content with the kind of purely negative attack upon present policies and institutions which we hear so often today. He will recognize that having rejected the *status quo,* he must present some better course of action. In a nuclear age, such an alternative proposal must offer some promise not only of getting us through next weekend with both our hides and our freedom intact; it must also contain the possibility of producing some long-term solution to the problem of atomic war.

An analysis of the contemporary situation in international life reveals two significant lines of development. One line leads toward heightened world tension, dispute, and hatred. The second line leads toward a constantly increasing quantity, destructiveness, and distribution of nuclear weapons among the nations. If we listen to the counsel of those who tell us to abandon the United Nations and its possibilities for reconciliation, cease any attempts at negotiated settlement of disputes, and reject any efforts to limit nuclear weapons and testing, we are left with little recourse except these two lines of development as the inevitable wave of the future. Under such circumstances, there is no other possibility than that, sooner or later, the two lines will intersect. The point at which they will intersect is a nuclear Armageddon, the nearest thing to the production of hell on earth that the mind of man can imagine.

Certainly, the United Nations, in itself, can make no concrete guarantee that the lines will not converge. No thinking man urges that the United States pin all its hope for survival on the United Nations, abandoning other instruments of national policy. But let us be very clear. If there is ever to be any workable world order, it will not come by international withdrawal and isolation, nor will it be produced by wishful thinking, half-baked rabble-rousing, or pious lip service to the cause of peace. A world of peace and order will come both slowly and painfully. The price will include sacrifice, hard work, constant trial and error. Our real hope is that, in the immediate future as in the past, we will somehow be able to "muddle through" a good many crises without blowing ourselves or somebody else into eternity. It appears that it will take a good while longer for most of us to learn, largely through unhappy experience, the realities of world power politics and our inescapable involvement in its machinations. Among other things, we must learn that patriotic platitudes are no substitute for the hard, complicated, complex, and thankless tasks of diplomacy.

More than any other group on earth, Christians ought to be those who, in the midst of all of this, without illusion or self-deception, still proclaim a message of hope. It is the Christian who understands that "this is our Father's world," and that he and his fellow believers are stewards of everything in that world, including its peace and order. If we can learn fast enough, work hard enough, pray sincerely enough, and exercise enough cool common sense and priceless patience, we *can* help to build a better world for ourselves, for our children, and for our grandchildren. The struggle is more concentrated and urgent than ever before, but it is basically the same old struggle with the same old adversary—the sin and evil in the hearts of men. In that struggle, all kinds of men have found themselves constrained to enlist, from a great variety of motivations. Christians, constrained by the love of God the Father, are not cut out to play the role of spectators. The United Nations is not a way of salvation. It is neither good nor evil within itself. It is a political mechanism representing the most advanced attempt the world's nations have made, up to this point, to create an international society of relative peace, order, and justice. It can be used wisely and effectively in the interest of peace. Christian citizens have an inescapable responsibility to use their influence to support its creative endeavors.

7.

THE UNITED NATIONS AND THE AMERICAN REVOLUTION IN HISTORICAL PERSPECTIVE

FRANK P. GRAHAM

United Nations Representative for India and Pakistan and for 19 years President of the University of North Carolina

(This is a transcription of an informal talk made without notes.)

I have just come from Nags Head, North Carolina, that little sand bar off the coast. My wife and I were there one August time on a vacation. One particular night one of the most terrific hurricanes that ever hit the Carolina shore broke through the little cottage in which we were staying. We, of course, had to get out of the cottage amid the surging waters and seek refuge in a cottage on higher ground. As we approached our neighbor's cottage, I saw a venerable cook in the kitchen. It was then toward sunrise, and it was reassuring to me, an uplander, that here was a woman of great faith who thought the world would at least last until breakfast time. So I went into her kitchen for further reassurance, and I said to her, "It seems to me that the ocean outside your kitchen window may be going down just a little bit." She turned to me with the wisdom of her years and said, "Mr. Graham, it ain't them little three feet of ocean outside my kitchen window that's bothering me. It's those 3,000 miles of ocean out there leaning up against those little three feet that's on my mind." And if that ocean had leaned just a little more I would never have made it back to high ground.

As we look at the world today, we see not only three feet, we see not only 3,000 miles, but we see 25,000 miles of problems and perils and hopes leaning across this earth up against the United Nations, which is at least one of the hopes of freedom and peace in our time. As the world leans up against the United Nations, the United Nations leans up against you. After all, the real foundations of the United Nations are not at 42nd Street and East River. Its real foundations are in the hearts and minds of people in the churches, in business enterprises, labor unions, farm organizations, women's organizations, etc. By the way, amid all the criticism of the churches about this and that, it is my observation that if it were not for the churches, and particularly the women of the churches, we would be in far greater trouble than we are in these United States today. This quiet work that is done in study groups and social action groups of the churches is one of the main sources of the strength, sanity, and spiritual hope in our present world. That is where the real foundations of the United Nations are today.

I'll give you an illustration of what going to the UN means in some cases. Some people for years have joined in that cry about getting the UN out of the United States or the United States out of the UN. Well, there were some farm women who heard about all these charges—that the UN was a center of Communism—and one farm woman said, "Let's go up there and find out." And they took their egg money and the money from canned fruits and vegetables, and one hundred of them from one hundred counties, under the leadership of this one woman, went to the United Nations. I happened to get in touch with them and so I can speak first-hand. They were all over the place—buying books, pamphlets, attending meetings, interviewing delegations, and so forth. Those one hundred farm women went back to North Carolina and made 1,000 talks on the United Nations. No senator or congressman has ever dared since to say to them, "Let's get the UN out of the United States." That is what one dedicated woman did.

Today the extreme right in America and the extreme left in

the world are in an unconscious alliance to paralyze the United Nations. I think it is necessary, in view of this double attack and this unconscious alliance of the two extremes against the UN, for us to try to see the UN in perspective. I will not stop here to talk about what the alternatives might be if we did not have a UN.

Let us see the UN in the perspective of depth and in the perspective of breadth. Let us take it first in the vertical perspective—that of depth. We know that man by nature has a capacity for good and evil. Atomic power in the hands of man has a capacity for both good and evil. Stored deep in the subconscious nature of man is a long inheritance as cruel savages and uncivilized barbarians. Only in relatively recent times has there been a deepening of the consciousness of God and the brotherhood of all people. Just as man by his very nature needs religion, the depth of his human predicament calls for the sublimation of the savage that is in his subconscious nature. Moreover, the absolute nation states need the United Nations for the guidance, control, and sublimation of this savage element. So we say that in the perspective of millions of years, the United Nations in the atomic age has become a moral imperative.

We are living in a time when there is potentially a juncture of this primitive power deep in the subconscious of man and this vast potential power that is deep in the nature of the atom itself. If we have a juncture of those two forces, uncontrolled or unguided by the religious and humane spirit and some such organization as the United Nations, that combined force of primitive savage power and this tremendous atomic power might break through this thin crust of civilization and bring an end to the human race. I think that we can say, therefore, that not only the churches but also the United Nations are moral imperatives in this atomic age.

So much for the perspective of hundreds of thousands of years. Suppose we come nearer to the last five thousand years. We witness the evolution of political states from tribal states to city states, to empire states, to feudal states of ancient and Medieval times, to the nation states of modern times. We are now confronted with a great alternative as to whether the next transition in the evolution of political states will be from the nation states to a totalitarian world, or, more hopefully and more creatively, to the more effective international cooperation of the nation states in a more adequate United Nations for the collective security of all men. In the perspective of man's long history, and particularly that of the last five thousand years, we must have the United Nations in this atomic age.

Let us come nearer to what we call the Modern Age. Here we become historical witnesses of three great economic revolutions. Five hundred years ago, when the world was turning from the Medieval to the Modern Age, one of its little pivots was the mariner's compass. Also at that time, in the Renaissance world, we were rediscovering the ancient world with the revival of learning. One of the ideas recovered was that the earth is round. The mind of man at that age was not only recovering old ideas, but it was also discovering new ideas. One of these ideas toward which the mind of man was groping was not only the old idea that the earth was round, but the new idea that the earth itself is a great magnet through which run electro-magnetic lines which you cannot even see, yet which are so powerful that a little needle pivoted in the mariner's compass would always point true north or south. This concept enabled Columbus to discover America and Vasco de Gama to round Africa by water to India, Indonesia, and the great East. An idea became a mechanism, the mechanism brought on the great revolution in the fifteenth, sixteenth, and seventeenth centuries, and this tied the world together in one commercially interdependent world, looking toward the day when the United Nations would become a necessity.

About three hundred years later, a professor in the University of Glasgow named Joseph Black did some very fundamental thinking and speculating about the latent power of heat. Joseph Black's laboratory assistant, James Watts, took his theory and mechanized it, putting the expansive power of steam behind a piston. This led to the modern steam-power engine. An idea became a mechanism, and the mechanism wrought the great Industrial Revolution, which on top of the Commercial Revolution tied this world even more tightly together in one commercially and industrially interdependent world. A Slavic youth in a remote village pulled a trigger, killing the Archduke of Austria. Of course, the pull of that trigger did not cause the first World War. We had come to live in a kind of world, however, when a trigger pulled at the crossroads of the world could precipitate and release such pent-up economic, social, psychological, political, and military forces that in less than four years two million American boys had crossed the ocean. Ten million of the finest youth in the world were killed on the battlefields of three continents.

It was in that kind of a world that these so-called theoretical, scientific, philosophical people in universities and research centers were speculating again. A woman at the University of Paris speculated that perhaps the atom, which for generations had been considered the ultimate particle of the universe, was itself a little universe made up of many components—a bundle of energy, protons, neutrons, electrons, whirling with unbelievable power. Such terrific power was enclosed in this tiny atom which you could not even see that if you could split it open, you might capture something like the power of the universe itself.

Again, an idea was mechanized. It was mechanized in reactors and bombs. This time it was not the idea of the electromagnetic nature of the earth or the latent power of heat and the expansive power of steam, but the idea of the nuclear nature of the atom. An idea was mechanized and the mechanism is working the tremendous Atomic Revolution, which on top of the Industrial Revolution, which on top of the Commercial Revolution, has tied this world tightly together in one commercially, industrially, fatefully, interdependent world. We Americans had to learn the hard way that we live in a kind of world in which there could never again be any isolation from the skies above, the seas around, or the continents beyond. These great power engines and mechanisms in their procession around this little globe called the earth, have built up such an earth-wide industrial, economic, and social structure that they could gather up a war or depression anywhere and involve human beings everywhere.

It is fortunate historically, providentially, and religiously, that in the very year in which atomic power made its entrance in history, the United Nations made its entrance on the stage of the world. We Americans decided that instead of staying on the outside and being drawn into these world wars after they are started, we would join the United Nations and at least try more effectively on the inside to prevent the beginnings of a third world war. You know, our splendid isolation between the two great ocean moats did not keep us out of the Second World War. Staying out of the League of Nations did not keep us out of the Second World War. Therefore, it was reasoned, we should work on the inside in an effort to prevent the third world war. A weak, frustrated United Nations without any great power except the moral power that the peoples of the churches and voluntary organizations and the citizens of the various nations of earth put into it, has nevertheless cooled off seven hot spots where a local fire might have become a global conflagration. By its very existence as a world forum, as a safety valve for the expression of grievances and the release of tension, the United Nations has accomplished great good. Some people say that the UN is just a talking society and does little good. What if this is all it is, a place where men shout at one another? Is it not better that the delegates of more than one hundred nations shout at each other than that more than one hundred million young people shoot at each other on the battlefields of the globe? By its very existence, the United Nations has so far prevented the beginning of the third world war. It needs for its own survival and the survival of the human race to grow in strength and in influence by some such measure as an international police force, by longer range and more intelligent economic development programs against mass misery, and by attempts to relieve these masses of their misery. There is also the need to keep up the incessant struggle for beginning steps in universal disarmament.

We have in the Nuclear Test Ban Treaty a beginning step toward disarmament. It is a very limited thing, but at least it is a beginning of what we hope will be a reciprocally developing faith. Its ratification by the United States Senate was a great thing for the world, an expression of faith and freedom. The alternative between a slight beginning and a total rejection might involve whether we are going to go the way of downward drift toward universal annihilation or the upward, patient struggle toward international cooperation. In view of its limited nature, why should we be so concerned about the test ban treaty? You make great decisions in making little decisions. Great decisions in historic times have come out of little decisions in cumulative times. The treaty must be and will be without any appeasement of totalitarian tyranny and without any surrender of the great goals of the eventual freedom and self-determination and peace of all peoples on the earth.

We Americans at this time need to make clear to the world where we stand with regard to the United Nations. There is a great backwash of opposition to the United Nations across this country. There is a slow, beginning attrition to try to wear down our faith in the little beginning which has been made.

It helps us also as we look worldward, at the same time to look homeward because the world is looking at us. There are a billion people in the totalitarian world and there are a billion people in what we like to call the free world. There are a billion people caught somewhere in between, looking East and West. In this crucial hour, they are looking at us for some signs of humane hope. If we signal to them that we don't have any faith in a little beginning, and if we signal to them that we are not going to be true to our own great American heritage set forth in the Declaration of Independence, their hopes will be directed elsewhere.

The American Declaration of Independence was the first universal declaration of human rights ever adopted by the delegates of the people. That great declaration and its ideas went winging around this earth, ringing down the years, and are still ringing in the hearts of the people of two hemispheres.

The Bandung Conference of Asian and African people met in 1955 representing some two billion people. They invited the world to come, but the Europeans and Americans could not come as delegates, only as observers. We were so afraid of being contaminated in that McCarthy period by just being near any Communist people that we would not even send an observer to Bandung. When the President of the Bandung Conference uttered his first sentence, do you know what he said? He said, "We meet today on the one hundred eighty-first anniversary of the midnight ride of Paul Revere, the beginning of the first successful revolt against colonialism in modern times." He planted his flag with the great idea that the American Declaration of Independence is the ideal, and we were not even there to observe. That illustrates that this tremendously revolutionary American idea that went around the world is still carrying on.

Surely when our own ideas have gone around the world and have come back again in the current Negro revolution, we are not going to reject now our own revolutionary heritage in the house of the Founding Fathers. America was the home of the disinherited of the earth, even the ancestors of the Daughters of the American Revolution. I have a sister who is one of their members, and I am all for the Daughters, especially in their humane programs. But I trust that the sons and daughters of the American Revolution will not become the fathers and mothers of a great American reaction against the very principles for which the American Revolution was fought. America, the home of a tremendous, revolutionary faith in the time of our infant weakness, should not now become in the days of our vast power the home of a paralyzing fear and a vastly destructive intolerance. We need to make clear to the world that our great declarations of human freedom and equality are not only the historic past, but are the present and living sources of America's faith in herself and America's moral influence in the world.

These American revolutionary ideas about equal dignity of all people, self-determination of all people, and separation of church and state have all come home to us today.

The important thing is whether or not we shall fulfill these ideals in providing freedom and justice to the Negro people. You know, Martin Luther King said that whenever you try to do something for the colored people someone always asks whether you want your sister to marry a Negro. He said, "I don't want to be your brother-in-law, I want to want to be your brother." And it is just that simple. These young Negro people did not get their start in Moscow. I do not know why we are always ascribing to the Communists some of the best things in our own religious heritage. That is a strange way to teach young people—that all our good things belong to the Communists. They belong to us. Years ahead, centuries ahead of the Communists, these ideals were ours. But if we keep ascribing them to the Communists, after a while the world will believe that all of these good things belong not to America but to Moscow.

We have recently been witnessing a movement by a minority group in our country to have the same service for the same price. These young people in sitting down were really standing up for the American dream. They were trying to obey the Constitution as against the local ordinance. They are not trying to overthrow the Republic, they are trying to fulfill the promise of the Republic. This movement did not get started in Moscow, it started in Greensboro, North Carolina, and Montgomery, Alabama. Where are its fundamental sources? Not only Greensboro and Montgomery and other cities of the Southland. This movement got started in Philadelphia, where the American people had a historic rendezvous for a great declaration of human rights.

Sometimes it is overlooked, but the movement began even before Montgomery and Philadelphia. Its farther headwaters are in the Judean hills and around the Sea of Galilee where the most radical person ever to walk the earth, Son of Man, Son of God, lived, preached, suffered, died, and triumphed over death for the equal dignity, freedom, equality, and sacredness of all persons as children of one God and brothers of all people. And is it not good for us in our times that the real leaders of this revolution updating the American Revolution, are not given to hate and violence? Suppose they organized a great nation-wide, secret conspiracy for violence and assassination during the nighttime as certain revolutionaries did in Santo Domingo. The leadership during the first critical years has been in the hands of religious people. With the Bible and the Constitution and the Bill of Rights in their hands, with prayers and hymns on their lips and nonviolence and brotherhood in their hearts, they are in the great Judeo-Christian tradition and in the great American revolutionary heritage. They seek equal freedom and self-determination under the law. There are going to be Communists seeking to infiltrate the movement, of course. Communists always try to infiltrate every good thing and then claim it as their own. Some of us make the mistake of surrendering it to them when it is really our own.

You see, what I am trying to do is to tie the United Nations, the test ban treaty, the American Revolution, and the Negro Revolution all together in one great Judeo-Christian, American, democratic, integrated whole. The spiritual leaders who pioneered this movement have reinforced my faith that the current civil rights revolution will reveal our best selves at home and a truer American image in the world.

The best representatives that America has today in Asia and Africa are the young Negroes. They are loyal Americans. In some sense, with their taking literally the meaning of the Sermon on the Mount, and the American Declaration of Independence, the Negroes are the most religious in faith and the most American in hope.

Who does not want to be a part of that struggle to make America a land where there is always the freedom to struggle for a higher freedom? We know that it cannot come overnight.

It has to come by larger and larger fulfillment of the American dream. We started out with a great declaration of human equality, but in many American states there was not much actual equality, either North or South. To vote and hold office you had to be a Protestant. You had to own land. You had to be white. And you had to be male. It took decades, even a century, to keep opening the doors for Jews and Catholics as well as for Protestants, landless people as well as propertied people, colored people as well as white people. And finally we got around to the women. Do you remember that the women used to have marches on Washington? They marched not only up Fifth Avenue but also up Pennsylvania Avenue. A lot of them got put in jail. At that time the women were considered the most subversive people on the earth, but finally we opened the doors to the women. Now we have great women leaders. It took the Jeffersonian, Jacksonian, Lincolnian, progressive eras to open these doors for all people. Until very recently, in some counties and some states the doors were not open when some people came up to register to vote. The recent effort to extend the voting privilege, however, has been a part of the continuing American revolution.

In this connection, let us consider briefly the theory of states' rights. One of the noble theories of our American system is that doctrine which provides in our federal structure a proper place for both the state and the nation. States' rights was a nobly conceived theory, and yet sometimes it has been overly used. When we got scared to death of the French Revolution and began to see Jacobins behind every bush and under every bed, we passed the Alien and Sedition laws and started throwing people in jail. This was especially true if they were followers of Thomas Jefferson! The authorities closed up newspapers that were speaking out too much. Thomas Jefferson was in retirement, but he came down out of the hills of Virginia to take up again a lifelong struggle for human freedom and human dignity. He mustered the people of this America across all state lines. He was a great states' rights man, but he organized the first national movement in our history against the Alien and Sedition laws, their federal tyranny, and their national hysteria. States' rights was a sword of liberty in Thomas Jefferson's hands. Then a little later states' rights became the shield of slavery. And then later when the basis of economic and political power shifted from plantation and slave labor in the South to the corporation and machine labor in the North, what did states' rights become? Northern people sometimes forget this, but they used states' rights for the protection of the exploitation of little children eight or ten years old, wearing their lives away fourteen hours a day for 4¢ an hour. This happened in the great sweatshops of the northern cities. What was the weapon that was used against Jane Addams, the daughter of an enlightened industrialist who tried to stand by these little children? What did they put in between her and the children? The theory of states' rights.

In more recent times, states' rights has become the armament of massive resistance to the civil rights movement in fulfillment of the Christian heritage and the American ideals. The doctrine of states' rights has great value, but let us not be deceived into misuing it against our own American heritage.

Right-thinking men everywhere would like to be a part of the movement to make America a land where there is always the freedom to struggle for higher freedom; where we would achieve democracy without vulgarity and excellence without arrogance; where the answer to error is not terror; where the response to a difference in color or race or religion or economic condition is not discrimination, exploitation, or intimidation; where the way of progress is certainly not subversion; where respect for the great past is not reaction and the hope for a greater future is not violent revolution; and where we would achieve our great goals both without tyranny of the majority and without the oppression of the minority.

May we rise to the responsibility of our power and the opportunity for our greatness to give fresh hopes of the good life and freedom to stricken peoples around this earth. In partnership with all peoples, may we work for a stronger United Nations and a more peaceful world. In this time when the panic-press of a button might end the human race, and in this world when the roads of human destiny fatefully cross, either in that downward drift toward universal annihilation or in that patient upward struggle toward more effective international cooperation through the United Nations, I express the faith and the hope that all Americans will become a part of the structure and substance of man's unresting dream of building on this earth a nobler home of the family of man. This is that eternal adventure of the human spirit toward equal freedom, justice, and peace under the law, and human brotherhood under God, which must be carried on in this time of moral peril and immortal hope for all people everywhere.

8.

MISSIONS AND PEACE

WILLIAM M. DYAL, JR.
Former Director of Organization
The Christian Life Commission of the
Southern Baptist Convention

The Christian mission today is to twentieth-century man. Nineteenth-century approaches will not suffice in this hour of world revolution. To evaluate the task of world Christian witness requires first of all an understanding of the context of witness. Self-criticism and insight are mandatory. The role of Christian missions as peacemaker in a hostile world must be re-examined.

Pull the blinds of provincialism aside and look at the world. Governor Luis Munoz Marin of Puerto Rico describes the four modern horsemen of the apocalypse as poverty, ignorance, disease, and tyranny. Until man comes to grips with these, he cannot hope to proclaim peace with any real effectiveness.

The sheer magnitude of hungry millions startles. Explosion of population continues. If all that faces this breeding mass of humanity is more poverty, their fury is going to rock the world. Their fury is being felt already. Edwin Markham prophesied that when the masses found their voices the world would be turned upside down.

> O masters, lords, and rulers
> of all lands,
> How will the Future reckon with
> this Man?

How answer his brute question
in that hour
When whirlwinds of rebellion shake
the world?
How will it be with kingdoms and
with kings—
With those who shaped him to the
thing he is—
When this dumb Terror shall reply
to God,
After the silence of the centuries?[1]

Our generation is witnessing the fulfillment of this prophecy.

This is an hour when new nations are being launched so rapidly that one gets the feel of a Cape Kennedy countdown. As nation after nation streaks off the launching pad, the question of its orbital ability is raised. Will it become another Kenya to take its place in the hall of nations with dignity, or will it become another chaotic Congo? We are deeply aware of the mass movements of men. Algeria, Vietnam, Angola, and South Africa fill the news media.

The context in which the Christian mission works is one of a depersonalization of man. Man has been made merely a machine, a robot, a statistic, or a sociological concept. The revulsion against war and bloodshed is thus diminished. If a man can be relegated to a state of machinery, his flesh and blood, his personality and dreams, and his misery and grandeur become inconsequential. He becomes a mere means to an end and not an end in himself.

Not only around the world but in his own homeland the missionary must understand the difficult context for his mission for the Prince of Peace. Away for four or five years he tends to idealize the United States. On his return, with a new-found objectivity, he senses that his countrymen have often allowed themselves to become extremely provincial. In the news of cold war power blocs, he hears a friend say, "Oh, well, why be concerned? God's on our side. He's on his throne." And the missionary is

[1]"The Man With the Hoe," Edwin Markham, *The Best Loved Poems of the American People,* Selected by Hazel Felleman (Garden City, New York: Garden City Books, 1936), p. 596.

compelled to answer, "Indeed, God is on his throne; but his throne is not located in Washington, D. C.!"

The missionary sees through the idea that because the United States may have a superior economy, it naturally follows that it has a superior culture. The missionary becomes aware of the juvenile way Americans tend to deal in absolutes as we approach our world. The United States is thought of as being absolutely right and our political enemies as absolutely wrong. Many Americans apparently believe that we possess the whole truth and God included! The American missionary becomes painfully aware that we are a people who have better communications systems than anyone in history, but live provincially and at times in tragic isolation. The status quo is saluted on all sides. We love slogans and themes and our religious convocations are generally headlined by them. If our real themes, the ones we live by, were stated, however, we would be shocked. One might be revealed: "Every Christian a Non-Boatrocker." The thought seems to be, "Never disturb the waters." Say nothing, do nothing, be nothing, that will cause a ripple. Many call this peace. In actuality it is a glossing of subsurface friction and disquietude.

As the missionary contemplates his task in this world he also must ask, "Does war affect my witness?" His answer is the answer of the German youth who said that war is an idiot who splits a violin to make firewood for his stove. War is always idiotic and always destructive. War for Christian missions is tragically divisive. War split families in Japan. War alienated and isolated Americans and Japanese as Christian brothers. War imprisoned and tortured Christian pastors and laymen in Germany because of their convictions. War locked church doors in China. Only the historians of the church of tomorrow will be able to tell the whole story of what war has done in China to the Christian churches. The book *Bill Wallace of China* is required reading for concerned Christians. Its portrayal of war's destruction of life and mission in Christ is appalling.

But war is also distorting. It causes man to stereotype his fellowman. War forces man to categorize the opponent, regardless of his personal quality, in beastly terms. The enemy cannot be killed unless he is hated, so the machinery of hate and enmity works overtime. If the opposing side can be reduced to an inferior level, or to a totally gross and immoral position, we can find justification for our hatred and for all the multiplied immoralities of war.

What is the missionary's role as a peacemaker in the midst of this kind of world? First, a definition of peace in this immediate context is necessary. Peace means far more than simply the absence of war. Peace which is genuine and lasting is always characterized by freedom, by justice, by truth, and by love. Peace is creative in nature. It is more than a proclamation. It is more than the resolutions we pass in our annual Christian gatherings. Resolutions without concerted peacemaking attitudes and actions are sounding brass. War cannot be destroyed merely by proclaiming peaceful goals. Too, peace is more than programing. A calendar full of activity promoting peace can still be pushed by a warring spirit. Peace requires not only doing something but being something. In this sense the missionary must become a personal embodiment of the quality of peace. He is still a man, capable of gross error as well as greatness. Yet, ideally the missionary is the human embodiment of Christ's matchless peacemaking.

The missionary is a *symbol* of peace. He is a symbol of the international and supernatural order in Christ. He is a symbol of a Christ who always breaks in from the outside, of a Saviour who comes as a foreigner, not from the United States but from the outer space of God's grace. True, the missionary never divorces himself from his own country, but he must be more a representative of Christ than of a political and cultural system.

The missionary is a *mediator* for peace. As mediator, he is a bridge-builder, constantly seeking to span the gulf between man and God and between man and man. In Christ, he bridges men divided by hatred, by misunderstanding, by race, by caste, by creed, and by culture.

Ideally, the missionary is also a *challenge* to peace. He embodies the challenge that is in Christ for a higher way of life. He witnesses to the challenge of the truth, the way, and the life which is found in the person of Christ and in His religion. The missionary represents this gospel of mediation and challenge. An illustration is found in Switzerland's International Baptist Seminary where roommates have discovered a common bond through Jesus Christ in spite of backgrounds of ancient national enmity. Arab and Jew, Frenchman and German live and study together. Here are men on a peaceful common ground unknown to them outside the Christian community. Such a challenge to an old order I have witnessed in the relationship between Mayan Indians and Spaniards in Guatemala. The Mayans have borne centuries of abuse as a conquered people. Though they are in the majority, the Spanish minority rules them and ostracizes them. Great hostility exists in both camps. Yet in the churches at times I, as a Christian missionary, have witnessed a breakthrough of Christian love between persons in the two cultures. Christ is the catalyst.

In even more specific terms, let us seek to determine the peacemaking task of Christian missions. Some basic theology is involved. Since God has created us in His own image, then the highest order or expression of His creation should reflect Him. God is Creator and Redeemer. Therefore, a witness of Him to our world must be creative and redemptive. This assertion needs further spelling out.

First, to be creative is to reassert in contemporary language that man is man. It is to establish this fact as against the depersonalization of man so prevalent in our time. It is to preach that man is more than a body, a brain, a customer, a producer, a voter, or a statistic. Doestoevsky reminds us that man is man and not the keys of a piano.

The creative ministry of the missionary is to prod men to ask the daring questions, "Who am I?" and "What does it mean to have a brain, to be a living soul, to have a zest for life?" The privilege of Christian missions is not only to prod man to ask this question, but to accompany him in his quest until he comes to the solution under God in Christ. The missionary's concern for the individual man's quest falls outside the framework of nation or political party or social system or mundane ideology. These are beside the point as man stands naked before God asking the tremendous question, "Who am I?" The Christian missionary's ministry is to help man find his identity, to help him discover his mind, and to help him explore the stretches of his own soul. A telling example of the difficulty of man's search for identity came in the words of a student from the Middle East. In conversation with me, he said, "I was born in a cradle of hostility and grew up on a diet of land mines, barbed wire, and violence. I shall probably marry and raise my children on the same diet, unless peace may come." Man must be given more than a cradle of hate and a diet of violence.

May God help us recover a sense of the personal quality and dignity of life He breathed into every soul on the face of the earth. There can be no peace which does not begin with this recovery. The missionary's ministry begins here. No matter how many streets he walks down or how many outstretched hands he sees, or how many faces blur in his memory, he must be drawn back every time to the one. He cannot talk about loving all unless he begins by loving the one. He cannot witness to all until he has dared through all language and culture barriers to witness to the one.

The creative peacemaker task of Christian missions also affirms that not only is man *man,* but that man has a destiny. Under God, man is capable of peace. Christian missions must keep alive the hope of a warless world. It must be a reminder to man that he may yet transform his weapons into instruments of human welfare.

At the same time, the gospel which talks about a peace characterized by freedom, justice, truth, and love is also a gospel of such radical nature that it inspires revolution to fulfill these characteristics. Wherever the doctrine of individual worth and soul liberty is proclaimed life will be changed. Not just personal life, but social and political life as well are involved. Peace without justice is no peace. Salazar, the dictator of Portugal, gave witness to this revolutionary gospel when he expelled some Protestant evangelical missionaries from Portuguese Angola. He condemned their Christian teachings as inflammatory, causing people to rebel against colonial rule without representative government and without equality of rights and opportunity. People held in obeisance for years are now demanding self-government. The *status quo* is being defied. What were the inflammatory teachings? Christ's teachings—that every man is God's creation and worthy of redemption.

We shall miss the full understanding of the impact of the Christian gospel in other lands if we fail to see its revolutionary character. A student from India complained to a group, "You Americans have long preached to the world in a vocabulary of words like democracy, freedom, and justice. You have talked about a God who is creator of all men and concerned with each man's welfare. Then when we take up the struggle to seek what you are talking about, you turn your backs on us and lose sympathy with us because too often our struggle seems to cut across your political and economic concerns." A telling indictment! The gospel of Jesus Christ is a force of such power that it cannot help but rip the seamless robe of the established order of sinful men. So it is that the gospel of Christ which would help a man discover who he is and what he should do with his life shall also be a gospel which comes often as a sword. Established order which defies justice for men and glosses over hatred between men is not acceptable. Peace without freedom and love is hollow.

The Christian mission is not only to be creative, then, but also redemptive. Missions is a ministry of reconciliation. The task of missions is to cross, with the gospel of Jesus Christ, every frontier between man and man, whether of race or class, caste or culture, tribe or tongue, nation or continent. The ministry of reconciliation recognizes the estrangement of man and God. Yet, how can one fathom the needs of men superstitiously fearful of evil spirits, of families split in rural to urban shifts, of the illiterate who are dependent on crafty rulers to interpret life for them, of people abused by race and caste cruelty, of students disenchanted with tyranny, of the hungry who have never known full barns nor bellies, or of empty men who have not known the loving Father of our Lord Jesus Christ? All of this produces misunderstanding, violence, and war.

Enter Christ! In the incarnation of God in Jesus Christ, the whole human race may recover the dignity of being made in the image of God. Through salvation, the incarnate Lord reminds us that we are brothers to our fellowmen. Because the Christian knows that God's reconciliation of the whole world is expressed in Christ, who is mankind's only real peace, he is free from the obsession with political security at all costs. He is willing to risk the important for that which is most important. He is aware that God is Lord of the universe, and he ceases to think of his own nation as a sanctified one and of his nation's wars as holy wars and of his nation's cause as absolute truth and good. He becomes deeply aware that God in Christ is God of all men. God thus shatters superiority complexes rooted in a particular nation, race, or culture.

Reconciliation is rooted in Christian love. There is no approaching this ministry without understanding love. The worst enemy of a man may be his own hate-touched soul. Jesus Christ always showed a radical preference for love over mere righteousness. His love is shockingly indiscriminate. His love reaches out to embrace the unembraceable, the ugly, the impure, and even the warlike spirit. To understand this is to understand the Christian missionary's approach to his world. Reconciliation begins at home, however. There are those in our churches who find no contradiction to Christian truth in giving to missions in Africa while despising and degrading the Negro in their own town. If reconciliation is sidetracked in the United States, it will be distorted abroad.

Also the redemptive ministry is concerned with building a fellowship in Christ. When men live in isolated camps set apart by superficial boundaries built by suspicion, hate will be the product. Where there is no communication, misunderstanding will grow. When men cannot see other men's pain and need, callous unconcern results. Through Jesus Christ and his reconciliation of man to man, Christian fellowship is extended from community to community, from race to race, and even from enemy to enemy. Side events in World War II dramatically expressed this unique fellowship. Numerous incidents were reported of American prisoners befriended by individual Christian Japanese soldiers. Other remarkable events were recorded of fliers who parachuted onto islands of the Pacific fearing primitive cannibalistic people only to discover Christian people who welcomed them and cared for them. This amazing strain of fellowship running through the world is a reminder of the Biblical concept of the "remnant." National leaders and aggressive, warring spirits are reminded that there is hope for peace while such a "remnant" exists and multiplies.

The best description of peace is the *agape* fellowship in Christ, a fellowship of love from Him, through Him, and for Him, with our fellows. John Bennett indicates that person-to-person relationships always transcend relationships between governments, classes, or races.[2] Where men as officials cannot get through to one another, men as men may make contact. The personal face-to-face ministry has no substitute. When that ministry is in the name of Christ, a unique common ground is established.

John Mackay spoke in 1957 to the Ghana Assembly of the International Missionary Council. He delivered a charge to Christendom which is still relevant: "Let the church proclaim that in human relations, even among enemies, there can be no substitute for personal confrontation under God in the spirit of Christ. Let the church shout aloud that civilization and all the nations that consider themselves to be civilized, stand in need of forgiveness. Let the church make unmistakably clear that even in international affairs, and despite the long record of failure around the conference table, there is still a place for the in-

[2]John C. Bennett, *When Christians Make Political Decisions* (New York: Reflection Book, Association Press, 1964), pp. 36-37.

junction of Jesus regarding a quality of patience and of forbearance in human relations, which involves a 'second mile' and the '70 times 7' of forgiveness."[3] Let the Christian remnant in every nation remind the state of peace and justice as live options.

The missionary then is involved in reconciliation and fellowship-building. His motivation thus is highly important. Why does he go? Personally, my own missionary pilgrimage of nearly ten years was a probing for this answer. I came to some clear conclusions. I did not go merely to wash from my hands the responsibility of other men's sin. I did not go primarily to win friends for the American way of life. I did not go to fight Communism, because I believe the good news about Christ is more than an offensive weapon. I did not go to engage in a lectureship to non-Christian religions, because I believe the gospel is addressed to persons rather than to religions. I did not go to transplant my culture lest I export to other lands some of the illnesses we have at home. I did not go in some vague humanitarian program. Nor did I go because my denomination is large and expansionistic.

I went because the world is what it has here been described as being, and because I believe the God who is at work in the world bade me link my life with Him there. I did not go to take Christ, for He was there before me. I sought to witness of Him, of His love for all men. A Costa Rican requested of me just before a furlough period that I tell my people that missionaries were still wanted, in spite of current anti-American sentiments. But he added, "Not just anyone. Tell them we need men who will come and give themselves to an understanding of our language and our culture, and also to our needs and our sin. We want men in Christ who will walk by our side, encourage and counsel us, until we are able in Christ to walk by the side of others in a like ministry."

God grant to us wisdom and determination that, not only

[3]Ronald Orchard (ed.), *The Ghana Assembly* (New York: Friendship Press, 1958), p. 122.

in our land, but in all the lands of the world we may have the love and courage to be such peacemakers. Let the voice of God be heard through his human instruments calling all men everywhere to faith. Let hope be sounded for a way of Peace. The Way is Jesus Christ.

9.

THE PLACE OF THE PEACE CORPS IN THE PEACE PICTURE

LLOYD WRIGHT
Former Director
Office of Public Affairs, Peace Corps
Washington, D. C.

When the Peace Corps began operation a few years ago, there was no textbook available on "How to Run a Peace Corps." There still isn't. But a fairly comprehensive handbook *could* be written now.

We've learned a lot about how to select the right type of people to represent the United States abroad, how to train them, how to support them in the field—even how volunteers should handle their correspondence home.

But the important lessons taught by the first years of Peace Corps experience are not the nuts and bolts of operating techniques. The basic lessons deal with the caliber of Americans our country is producing, the spirit that dwells within them, and the proper approaches to helping people in critical need of help.

If the Peace Corps today can be included among the things that make for peace, it is simply because skilled, dedicated Americans have been able to go abroad to do needed jobs, and in the doing of those jobs have transmitted the spirit of America.

"The Place of the Peace Corps in the Peace Picture" today has been painted by non-professional artists. But what started as an abstraction has now taken on the sharp lines of realism.

At the outset, we were not without critics. "A boondoggle," some cried. "Dewy-eyed idealists," they labeled our Volunteers. "Do-gooders in button-down shirts and bermuda shorts."

Because we were painting on a new canvas, using techniques untried before by any government agency, our basic policies were hammered out in long, detailed discussions in which we sought to face up to the practical problems and reach specific solutions before we actually started operations.

Even the choice of a name took on serious overtones. The phrase "Peace Corps" was used in the original San Francisco speech by President Kennedy, but many advisers disliked it. "Peace," they claimed, was a word the Communists had pre-empted, and "Corps" carried undesirable military connotations. We did not want a name contrived out of initials which a public relations firm might have devised; nor did we want to restrict participation in the program by calling it a "Youth Corps." What we did want was a name which the public at large could grasp emotionally as well as intellectually. Whatever name was chosen would be given content by our acts and programs. The initial small staff studied dozens of other names and finally came back to the original. Peace is the fundamental goal of our times. They believed the Peace Corps could contribute to its attainment, for while armaments can deter war, only men can create peace.

The ambitiousness of the name, of course, was only one reason for early skepticism about the Peace Corps. Fears were voiced that it might be a second "Children's Crusade." Apparently we had forgotten the earlier accomplishments of young men. Thomas Jefferson drafted the Declaration of Independence at thirty-three. Napoleon conquered Italy at twenty-five. Alexander the Great made most of his great military victories while in his twenties. He founded the city of Alexandria when twenty-four.

Forgotten also was the fact that more than half of the world's population is under twenty-six, the age of the average Peace Corps Volunteer. Many of the nations in Africa have heads of state under forty-five. Several have leaders in their thirties.

Americans—young and old—did respond to the Peace Corps challenge. More than 200,000 have written to volunteer their services. Those selected and sent overseas through 1966 (nearly 13,000 now working in 52 developing nations) have given a positive answer to the question in many early critics' minds: "Could Americans survive overseas without special foods, special privileges, special housing, automobiles, television, air conditioners, and motorized toothbrushes?"

Among our early critics were many church leaders who felt that the government was moving into a competitive program with their own mission efforts. We sought advice and experience of missionary leaders in those days. And today I think the experience of the Peace Corps provides encouraging news to the churches of our land.

Spiritual fervor is not on the wane, as many had begun to fear. Dedication is not lacking. Provide an accessible channel for serving worthy causes, and the response is overwhelming.

As a result of the response to the Peace Corps challenge by people of all faiths, several church groups have now moved to expand their own missionary programs to provide for short-term service opportunities for laymen and women. Others are launching such programs for the first time.

Instead of merely listening to sermons preaching the ideal of Christian love and brotherhood, thousands of our people are now offered the opportunity to work concretely toward it. And this opportunity is open to many who could never qualify by training, temperament, or circumstance to be missionaries in the normal sense; to many who may prefer to serve out of a pure desire to serve, without the underlying motive of converting members to Christianity.

By sponsoring the Peace Corps, the United States government is not taking over a church function. There is more work to be done in this world than any one group can do. The Peace Corps is trying to show that our nation's desire to help less fortunate people is not solely a materialistic one; that it is not based on selfish motives in a clash of ideologies.

"The Peace Corps," wrote Father R. J. Henle, Vice President of St. Louis University, "is giving Latin America a new view of the United States. They see love instead of power."

Robert E. Berry, a physician at the United Mission Hospital in Katmandu, Nepal, who treated Dr. William Unsoeld after he had participated in the recent American conquest of Mt. Everest, said in a letter to Sargent Shriver, who was then Director of the Peace Corps:

> "One of the satisfying experiences I have encountered in Nepal has been my association with the Peace Corps officers and Volunteers. Prior to this association, the Peace Corps to me was an idea or a program. Since I have seen them at work in their various jobs and under conditions which frequently are at best difficult, my respect for these individuals and for the work which they are doing is unlimited. One of the things which impresses me most is that in a country such as this, the only resources which are available to many of the Volunteers are the resources which they have within themselves, and frequently these young people have shown their resources to be ingenious and seemingly unlimited. Without hesitancy, I feel that these people are missionaries, though as Dr. Tracey K. Jones, Jr., stated in his recent book *Our Mission Today,* they do not fit the traditional image of what a missionary should be. Actually, this is fortunate. The Volunteers, however, have as the basis of their work the genuine trait of selfless giving, which is to me the fundamental prerequisite for any missionary."

The Peace Corps appeals to people who have been endowed either formally or informally with the same ideals of service as those which are preached from our pulpits.

When asked why they want to join the Peace Corps, the overwhelming majority of Volunteers give answers such as these: to help people; to work for brotherhood; to work for peace; to help make this a better world.

Whether they acquire these views in a simple Quaker meeting-house, in a Jewish synagogue, in a Unitarian lecture hall, in a Baptist revival meeting, in the woods of Thoreau, or simply from ethical instinct—the net result is that they feel an obligation to help their fellowmen, and they want to serve.

One applicant wrote: "I also hope to find some sort of personal peace, to salve my conscience that I and my peers were born between clean sheets when others were issued into the dust with a birthright of hunger. Perhaps afterwards when I hear the cry of humanity, I shall be unashamed that I am not of that cry because I helped to still a part of it."

Thus the idea behind the Peace Corps has meant for many a rebirth of the real meaning of the religious message. Perhaps the people are ahead of their religious leaders in many ways—they are rushing to perform the tasks of Christianity, regardless of their creeds. The churches worry about failure to grow as fast as they think they should. Perhaps their potential members scorn the dogmatic and sometimes petty divisions and differences and seek more direct ways to embrace the essence of the Christian message.

As a channel for serving all mankind, the Peace Corps has appealed to people of all faiths, backgrounds, persuasions, races, ages and educational levels. In the Peace Corps they have found a model in miniature of that fellowship of heart and hand aimed at overcoming what Historian Arnold Toynbee termed "the disastrous barriers that have hitherto segregated the affluent Western minority of the human race from the majority of their fellow men and women." Toynbee said: "I believe that in the Peace Corps, the non-Western majority of mankind is going to meet a sample of the Western man at his best."

The barrier-breaking begins with our staff and our Volunteers. We have working in the Peace Corps men and women of white skin, of yellow skin, of black skin, and of red skin. There are Protestants and Catholics, Jews and agnostics, farmers, mechanics, nurses, and Ph.D.'s.

The first two Volunteers to be killed on the job were a Jew and a Protestant. They died in a Catholic country, and the Bishop who consecrated their deaths called them "Martyrs."

We have Peace Corps Volunteers of all faiths teaching in Catholic mission schools abroad.

We have Peace Corps Volunteers of all faiths teaching in Protestant mission schools.

We have Peace Corps Volunteers of all faiths teaching in Buddhist schools. (None teach religious subjects, of course.)

We have Jewish Volunteers working in Moslem countries; Protestants working in Catholic countries; and Catholics laboring among pagan tribesmen.

And of all the thousands of Volunteers working in diverse countries, there has not been one single instance of racial or religious clash—not one instance in which belief has interfered with the day's work.

This is part of the mounting evidence that Volunteers of all faiths are learning to live and work with host-country nationals of different faiths.

Yet, at every step of the way in our planning, we were met with the warnings of the timid.

"Don't send Negroes to Africa," we were advised. "The Africans will think you are condescending."

"You can't send Jews to Tunisia and Morocco."

"You can't send Puerto Ricans to Latin America because 'they' look on Puerto Rico as an American Colony."

But the fact of the matter is that compassion and a sincere desire to serve can dissolve obstacles of race or belief anywhere in the world. People are hungry for contact, for understanding, for fellowship, for the breaking down of barriers.

True peace can come only when there is personal peace—not hate, distrust, suspicion—within individuals and among people.

That is why the place of the Peace Corps in the peace picture is so closely related to the role of the church. Both are concerned with helping *people,* not in providing things.

Talk about freedom, and peace, and building democratic institutions, has a hollow ring to a man whose family is starving. To provide teachers for students whose minds are numb from hunger and disease is not enough. You must wed education with improved health and sanitation.

To provide machines for industry is not enough. People must be developed and trained to use them. To provide techniques for improved agricultural production is not enough. Markets and distribution systems must be developed at the same time. We are convinced that economic development directly depends on social development. In his valedictory report as head of the Economic Commission for Latin America, Paul Prebisch observed that there are not "grounds for expecting that economic development will take place first and be followed in the natural course of events by social development. Both social and economic development must be achieved in measures that require the exercise of rational and deliberate action. . . . There can be no speed-up of economic development without a change in the social structure."

Notwithstanding the Peace Corps's primary emphasis on social development, Volunteers are making a direct economic contribution in a variety of situations. They are helping to organize farmers' cooperatives in Chile, Ecuador, and Pakistan; credit unions and savings and loan associations in Latin America; demonstration farms in the Near East. A group of Volunteers in the Punjab sparked the creation of a poultry industry of some economic significance, using ground termite mounds for protein feed. These are grass roots projects. More of them will some day cause us to look back and wonder why it took so long to discover that people—human hands and human enthusiasm—are an essential part of the relationship of mutual assistance which we must establish with our neighbors abroad.

A Jamaican radio commentator recently said that "a great distance between people is the best creator of good will. Jumble people up together on a sort of temporary basis of gratitude on one side and condescension on the other, and you'll have everyone at each other's throat in no time." If we believed this were inevitable, regardless of the attitude, preparation, and mode of life of Volunteers, we would disband the Peace Corps. But we have greater faith in the universality of men's aspirations and of men's ability to respect each other when they know each other. It is the American who lives abroad in isolation and the thoughtless tourist who create distrust and dislike.

We are already achieving in good measure all three of our Peace Corps objectives—providing needed middle-level manpower, helping people abroad better to understand America and

Americans, and improving America's understanding of the people abroad. As Peace Corps Volunteers are returning to take up their productive roles in our society, they are having a most positive influence, transmitting to other Americans their improved attitude and understanding of other people. American schools and students also benefit from the Peace Corps's initiative in another fashion. Two countries, Ghana and Argentina, have expressed interest in making the Peace Corps a two-way street by sending Volunteer teachers of special competence to interested American high schools or colleges. Ghana would provide experts in African history, and Argentina, teachers of Spanish. Other countries may follow suit.

Our own Peace Corps Volunteers are being changed in ways other than in the acquisition of languages and certain practical expertise. They will be coming home more mature, with a new outlook toward life and work.

Like many other Americans, I have wondered whether our contemporary society can continue to produce the self-reliance, initiative, and independence that we consider to be a part of our heritage. We have been in danger of losing ourselves among the television commercials and tranquilizers.

Both as a nation and as a demonstration of our plush way of living, our abundance has sapped the fervor of our faith.

It is in order here to refer to a statement by Yevgeny Yevtushenko, the Soviet poet who today exercises profound influence among millions of the world's captive people.

". . . It is the more fortunate nations, those favored by their geographical position and historical circumstances, that today show a grosser spirit and a weaker hold on moral principles.

"Nor would I call those nations happy despite all the signs of their prosperity. Never has the Biblical saying, 'Man does not live by bread alone' had such a ring of truth as it does today!

"Some great thinker once said that man is an animal with a capacity for dreaming," Yevtushenko writes. "There are men whose lives confirm only the first part of this proposition. Yet if we look into their hearts we find that, although they have no lofty dreams, there are dreams nevertheless, for man has a need to dream.

"However prosperous, a man will always be dissatisfied if he has no high ideal. And, whatever devices he may use to conceal his dissatisfaction even from himself, these will only make him feel more dissatisfied.

"But if even the rich feel burdened by the lack of an ideal, to those who suffer real deprivation an ideal is a first necessity of life. Where there is plenty of bread and a shortage of ideals, bread is no substitute for an ideal. But where bread is short, ideals are bread."

Why is it that a few radical extremists in our midst today can so confidently offer dogmatic solutions to cold war problems? Probably because "ignorance is bliss." They speak from a force-fed knowledge of an out-of-date history book. Most are unaware of the aspirations of people behind the iron curtain—aspirations given voice by men like Yevtushenko. To them, war and peace are mere words without real meaning. But, says Yevtushenko:

"The word 'peace' can have a concrete meaning only for those who know what war is. If it were possible to be grateful to a war, I would thank the war for giving men an understanding of the word 'peace'."

And what gives Communism its appeal? Let Yevtushenko answer.

". . . We have paid for our ideal with so much blood and torment that the cost itself has endeared it and made it more precious to us, as a child born in pain is more precious to its mother.

"You may say," he writes, " 'But doesn't it occur to you that Communism itself may be a false ideal?'

"If the reader believes in God I will ask him, 'Can you equate the substance of the Christian religion with the swindlers who used to make a handsome profit by selling indulgences, with the inquisitors, the priests who got rich at their parishioners' expense, or parishioners who pray piously in church and double-deal outside its walls?'

"Neither can I, a believing Communist," he says, "equate the essence of my religion with the crooks who climb on its bandwagon, with its inquisitors, its crafty, avaricious priests, or its double-dealing, double-faced parishioners.

"For me a Communist is not merely someone who belongs to the organization and pays his dues. A Communist is a man who puts the people's interests above his own, but who at the same time would never wantonly squander human lives in the name of those interests."

Neither today is a good American a smug, unconcerned, brash individual. To thousands of the world's struggling people today, an American is a concerned, sharing person, willing to get his hands dirty, joining them in their struggle to achieve dignity and economic progress, a Peace Corps Volunteer.

About some of his countrymen who are Communist in word only, Yevtushenko says: "Gradually it dawned on me that many people who called themselves Communists and eagerly quoted Lenin and Stalin at every opportunity were in reality not Communists at all.

"For these people, having party membership cards in their pockets and talking about Communism were simply ways of getting ahead and had nothing to do with their ideological convictions."[1]

Edit that statement slightly, changing "Communists" to "Christians," "Lenin and Stalin" to "Matthew and Mark" and you have an indictment that might well fit into any Sunday sermon.

Americans who are matching their convictions with deeds are painting a picture of a new American overseas today.

In an article written for *Foreign Affairs,* Sargent Shriver described the influence of the Peace Corps idea as a series of widening circles, like the expanding rings from a stone thrown into a pond. The inner, most sharply defined circle represents the immediate effect of the program's accomplishments abroad.

---

[1]From the book *A Precious Autobiography* by Yevgeny Yevtushenko. Copyright © 1963 by E. P. Dutton & Co., Inc. Reprinted by permission of the publisher.

The second ring moving outward on the water might be the Peace Corps influence on our society, on institutions and people, on the creation of a new sense of participation in world events, an influence on the national sense of purpose, self-reliance and an expanded concept of Volunteer service in time of peace.

There is still a wider circle, and, being farthest from the splash, the hardest to make out clearly. "Perhaps I can expain it," Mr. Shriver wrote, "by describing the relationships I see between the Peace Corps and our American Revolution. The Revolution placed on our citizens the responsibility for reordering their own social structure. It was a triumph over the idea that man is incompetent or incapable of shaping his destiny. It was our declaration of the irresistible strength of a universal idea connected with religious liberty, human dignity, hope, compassion and freedom. The idea was not simply American, of course, but arose from the confluence of history, geography and the genius of a resolute few at Philadelphia.

"We still have our vision, but our society has been drifting away from the world's majority; the young and raw, the colored, the hungry, and the oppressed. The Peace Corps is helping to put us again where we belong. It is our newest hope for rejoining the majority of the world without at the same time betraying our cultural, historic, political and spiritual ancestors and allies," he said.

It is not enough to be a son or daughter of the American revolution. We must be parents, propagators of American revolutionary doctrine. The world wants this great American revolution, not the monolithic, authoritarian, compulsory systems of Communism or Fascism. The world wants the vision of the free society created by Washington and Jefferson, Jackson and Lincoln, Wilson and Roosevelt. The heart of that vision was well expressed by John Quincy Adams in 1821 when he said:

"America, in the assembly of nations, has uniformly spoken among them the language of equal liberty, equal justice, and equal rights." No racial, political, religious, national or geographical barriers were applied by John Quincy Adams to the belief that "all men are created equal." This was a universal truth, applicable to every man, everywhere.

These American principles have swept all over the modern world. In new, young nations you see slogans scrawled in English on the walls of buildings, "Give me liberty or give me death" and "All men are created equal."

The people of these countries want the same objectives we have pursued for two hundred years: Life, Liberty, the Pursuit of Happiness, the Consent of the Governed, the Right of the People.

These ambitions of former colonial peoples offer an unprecedented opportunity to America. Never before has there been a time in which scores of nations were asking one nation for the spirit of its own free, democratic revolution.

An associate of Mahatma Ghandi told Mr. Shriver in India: "Yours was the first successful revolution for the common man in modern times. Your Peace Corps must touch the idealism of America and bring *that* to us. Can you do it?"

That's the true place of the Peace Corps in the peace picture—improving human understanding, helping create a climate in which peace can become a reality. Pablo Casals, the renowned cellist, said of the Peace Corps: "This is new, and it is also very old. We have come from the tyranny of the enormous, awesome, discordant machine, back to the realization that the beginning and the end are man—that it is man who is important, not the machine, and that it is man who accounts for growth, not just dollars and factories. Above all, that it is man who is the object of all our efforts."

Early critics, I said, thought our Volunteers would be dewy-eyed idealists. Listen to what a young Volunteer from Colorado said about his work:

> Agriculture is one of the greatest problems these people have. They plow with oxen, plant with sticks and poles, harvest by hand and use the winds to do their threshing. They farm on fields that have a 70 degree angle. I have seen women and children carrying water one or two miles up the side of a mountain to their mud huts. No matter

> what I say about the conditions, it's wonderful here. I'm having an experience most rewarding and know that I will not fully appreciate it for years to come. Perhaps you at home might understand a little about the problem. But until you see a mother following the funeral of her infant child, or searching through the trash for a pair of discarded shoes, . . . all the words in the world, put on paper by the best writer cannot describe the feeling I have developed for these people. It may seem futile to believe that 62 Peace Corps Volunteers can have any effect on the conditions here. But we will try and try harder than ever before. It takes *understanding*, patience, and hard work.

If that's dewy-eyed idealism, I say the world could use more of it!

10.

BLESSED ARE THE PEACEMAKERS

J. P. Allen
Pastor
Broadway Baptist Church
Fort Worth, Texas

In the quest for peace, there can be only one beginning. After that other vistas open up. And who of us is so inured against hope and so disillusioned by defeat that there is no quickening pace at the vision of peace on earth and men of good will?

The Imperative of Sonship to God

William Barclay, in his commentary on Matthew, paraphrases the seventh beatitude, "Oh, the bliss of those who produce right relationships between man and man, for they are doing a Godlike work." This is the force of the Hebrew's honored word for "peace"—*shalom*—and his characteristic term for benevolent greeting. Such address to a brother does not merely imply the absence of trouble, but the presence of everything which makes for his highest good.

The Jewish rabbis held that the highest task a man can perform is to establish right relationships between men. Then, as now, there are people who are storm centers of bitterness and strife. They change and charge the atmosphere about them. Witness the deacon who vowed, "As long as I am a member of this church, ain't nothing ever going to be unanimous." There are others who appear to have healing balm; bitterness cannot live in their presence; the breaches are healed. These are doing a Godlike work. They are doing what God does characteristically. They are akin to the divine nature, which nature is unremittingly committed to reconciliation.

A peacemaker, therefore, is called a son of God—again a Hebrew mode of expression. Not being rich in adjectives (which we have in vast superfluity) they referred not to a "comforting man" but a "son of consolation"; not to an embittered man but "son of bitterness." Such a trait would be inherent in his nature.

Indeed, no other nature has the capacity to produce peace save that which God can produce in men. Humanity is divisive, not unitive; full of self-assertiveness, not self-giving; possessive, not rich in healing grace. Unregenerate human nature is neither peaceful nor peaceable. All hopes are vain, therefore, which cry, "change the conditions," and then wait for a multitude of economic, political, and mechanical saviors to redeem the race. The Christian message is change the man, regenerate his nature. Thus transformed, there is some expectancy of men who know peace becoming makers of peace.

This is the essence of practicality! If a physics student in a laboratory finds the sifting of iron filings will not fall into polarity on the magnetic field in the experiment, he has no real alternative. He need not try with tweezers to force each filing into the expected pattern. It will not help to change the temperature in the room. Nor will cleansing each piece with a bath or staining each a different color prove practical. The lab instructor will inform him that all he need do is change the nature of the filings by changing their magnetic charge—as from negative to positive. It is not a matter as between a practical or impractical method. It is between the only way to do it or permanent, hopeless disarrangement of circumstances and environment.

Peace and peacemakers are God's arrangement. Without His regeneration, man is set irrevocably against the olive branch and the dove. His basic sin is pride! The center of sin is not in the lower nature of his appetites but in the higher center of personality—rebellion. Man wants to be God, without love as God loves. Even in his power God never violates human personality. When man arrogates power he destroys man. The Nazis inscribed over the gates of Offenbach, "Here is no God." They were right, for in himself man is diabolic.

There is something in human nature which resists love. Freud once declared love to be the first and all-consuming passion of life that will not be denied. Later clinical studies, however, caused him to revise that view to include another drive equally strong which he called the death instinct (thanatos) in opposition to the life instinct (eros). This theory has gained increasing confirmation.[1] Psychologists have found three basic emotions in the infant —fear, love and rage. In rage, a baby is no weakling. He screams, writhes, turns red with swollen circulation, strikes viciously against any restraint. Tantrums follow in childhood, and bursts of anger at every age take destructive forms.[2]

Any view of nature or society is naive and utopian that overlooks these aggressive trends. All is not sweetness and light in the souls of men. There are darker moods of sullen disdain and smoldering resentment. There are lurid explosions of blazing anger that lash out recklessly to destroy every value no matter how costly, how laboriously acquired, or how highly cherished at that moment.

Indeed, history's pages are reference material on the defeat of love in the social order; the strange and destructive impulse to hate and kill, the impulsion to deprive others even at our own expense, to have our revenge even if we all perish together, to wreck what we have built in a fiendish joy of destruction, and to die in the ruins of all we once cherished so dearly. G. K. Chesterton has said, "There is a spirit which drives men incessantly on to destroy what they cannot understand; to capture what they cannot enjoy."

Change man's nature, therefore! Do not seek to tame him,

---

[1]See Karl Meninger in his *Man Against Himself*.

[2]See Paul Emanuel Johnson, *Christian Love*(Nashville: Abingdon-Cokesbury, 1951), pp. 167 ff.

or merely organize him. Whoever aspires to walk any practical path to peace must begin here. The way is hard. Christ warned that it would be. Laborious it may be—practical it certainly is!

The Clamor for a World Consciousness

It is axiomatic that one's glory may become his peril. A denomination which finds its strength in its position on the requirement of the new birth experiences also the risk of getting lost in the drama and machinery of obstetrics. So much talk about being born again has left too little time for concern about the making of men. This is the New Testament major; and frequently our minor! Worse than the desire to be carried to the skies on flowery beds of ease is the wish to make the trip in a crib. Someone has reminded us that it was when Moses was grown that he looked upon the burdens of his people.

There is a positive clamor for Christians to grow up to a deliberate world awareness and involvement. Let no one take refuge behind our boasted missionary enterprises when it takes thousands upon thousands of church members' combined support to put one missionary on a foreign field, and the per capita gift to foreign missions is measured not in dollars but in dimes per annum! These are not accusations but assessments! It is one of the things we *can* do—force ourselves out of infantile provincialism into the adult world of dangerous responsibility!

Our denominational folkways have thought to save us from only the bottom rung of a ladder which ought to lure us to broader vistas. That ladder serves to illustrate how our climb upward out of self to the role of peacemaker is analogous to the ascent of mankind in his basic attitudes toward his fellow man. Once his appropriate term was *extermination.* Man or tribe looked upon his enemy, moved against him, and eliminated him with axe or spear. Later he climbed to a second rung, *exploitation.* He did not slay the foe, he captured him and sold him into slavery. A third step upward brought him to *toleration.* He neither slew nor enslaved, he merely bore him as a necessary burden. When he rose to the fourth level he reached *apprecia-*

tion. He began to understand and be moved by what was in the other man's heart. At the top is *cooperation*—acting together, living harmoniously.

In true fashion, men still run the same cycle. There are people who yet *exterminate* their enemies. Ruthless slaughter shocks us, but it is still with us. We are sure we have been saved from such gross sin! Fewer claim deliverance from *exploitation.* There are increasing devices to use personality. In this supposed advanced age, men still have dollar marks upon them; and America, generally, has social and economic morality by congressional investigation. The third rung, *toleration,* is densely populated. Indeed, attempts have been made to declare it Christianized. This is the prevailing mood, in the church and out of it. "Live and let live" sounds plausible if one does not think on it. It is a particularly apt refuge from disturbing racial adjustments. "Why, I do not *hate* Negroes" is heard all over. *Appreciation* is rarefied atmosphere and few there be who breathe it. It hurts to have "your pain in my heart." One is exposed to all sorts of claims upon himself if he identifies with others, for he might have to go, or give, or understand an enemy, or even try to affect reconciliation between enemies. It could even lead to *cooperation,* life's highest capability. This spiritual maturity was the goal for which the first moment of saving faith in Christ began to prepare. Man is born again so he can learn to live in ways which are Godlike. Such sons of God characteristically seek peace—right relationships between men, desiring their highest good.

This kind of spiritual adulthood, with this kind of salvation concept, will be able to operate with others without the price tag of agreement and outside the bargain basement of "one's own kind." Denominational provincialism and isolation closes the doors to involvement with others from the inside—the worst kind of closed doors. It is infantile to refuse cooperation with all except those with whom we agree. Christian denominations do not always and interminably need each other, but we do need dialogue with those outside our churches. No matter how fluently we articulate the beloved phrases of our own experience, we cannot speak the language of Zion to those who are not citizens of Zion (or even those who are not of our kind on the south side, or the north side, of Zion). And it is precisely these to whom we have been commissioned to go and "become all things to all men" if so be we might be able to save some of them. Why can one group of Christians not send fraternal messengers to any other conference or council of Christians who meet anywhere in the world to seek peace or confront social issues or face the moral judgments of our complex era? We need sacrifice no principle nor forfeit an iota of autonomy. We can recognize others—because they are there! We can listen and learn. We can deliberately step into broader world influence. We can agree when we can agree, and we can disagree without petulance when we must disagree. This is the role of *men* who would reconcile other men!

Perhaps a more pressing problem of provincialism is revealed on a national scale, and we are a part of the problem. When people behave the way nations behave, we put them away—either in prisons or in mental institutions. No society permits its individuals to act in arbitrary, irrational, or dangerous ways. There can be no peace in the world until the same law that applies to individuals applies also to nations. No matter how many treaties we make, how sound the alliances we form, or how many conferences we attend, so long as each nation is a law unto itself, the world can have at best only an uneasy truce.

How long could mankind have even a village if each villager refused to obey a common law, if he held himself a sovereign power, if he declared it his right to wage war on his neighbor whenever he saw fit? Yet the world today is as small as a village and far more inflammable. But we do not have a common police department, a common fire department, or a common court.

What is insane about this situation is not that it exists or that its existence is admitted by everyone, but that everyone persists in behaving as though it did not exist. What we call madness in the individual we call statecraft in the assembly of nations.

Christians today stand precariously with one foot in the eighteenth century and the other in the twentieth. We behave as though minutemen with muskets were defending Bunker Hill. Our social and political concepts are a mass of outmoded superstitions and slogans. The prime task is psychological, and this may be what makes the issue practical. *We can* change our minds. Government can change its mind. We can accept the cataclysmic changes in our world and correspondingly yield in the area of national autonomy. The single nation or even the alliance of a few nations is now as outmoded as the medieval duchy. Wars can no longer be won by powers or combinations of powers, for wars can no longer by won!

Men who aspire to promote peace can force their minds to a world consciousness that yields some cherished prerogatives and submits national sovereignty to the necessary limitations of cooperation with other peoples. The attitude is vital. The world ought to know that the sons of reconciliation are available to the council chamber, that they are willing to reason together, and even to give up what one may have that all may live.

The Challenge to Worthy Issues

A legend inscribed on the wall of the Old South Meeting House in Boston reads: "They were worthy to raise issues." Here was a church who construed issues as being of broader scope than doctrinal dissertation. They involved themselves in the rights of men, the nature of government, and the destiny of nations.

Would that we were worthy to raise issues; and raise worthy issues! Oh, the peril of the picayune. Jonathan Swift pictured Dr. Gulliver imprisoned by the threads of the Lilliputians, who flourished their swords the size of pins and set their spears very much like needles. The armaments of countless Christians today look something like that of these intrepid warriors. The church suffers very little by spear thrusts from without, but receives her mortal wound by pin thrusts from within. We have not even yet learned not to major on minors.

Christian churches have something to say about peace—even world peace. We are not such neophytes at global affairs as some would suggest. From its beginning Christianity lived in the arena of governments and the affairs of the state. A world religion properly has international implications. Indeed peace *is* our business, more even than that of the Congress of the United States or the Assembly of the United Nations. All is but truce or stalemate when men seek peace who have neither the Man of peace nor the message of peace.

It is easy to protest that we have no voice that may be heard. Yet a way was found to raise the issue of Catholicism and the American presidency. Outcries *are* heard when the subject of an envoy to the Vatican is mentioned. Affairs of church and state encroachment receive effective attention, and the weight of church opinion has been felt by many a local and federal government. American churches today have the publications, the commissions and the personnel to raise worthy issues—had we the conviction and the courage.

The Christian must raise the issue of *justice*. A peace settled or enforced on injustice is the same in effect as the solution of the Roman legions, "They made a desolation and called it peace." It is based on no foundation of reality and the evil fruit of bad seed is but postponed until the harvest will be more cataclysmic.

Would it be, for instance, both morally right *and* practical for Christian citizens to agitate for American espousal of the cause of the little people of the world as against the erstwhile "colonial powers"? As a nation which arose out of one of the most significant revolutions in world history, why should we not be on the side of continuing revolution? This is one stick of thunder the Communists ought not be allowed to steal from us. The new nations, carved largely from once-submerged masses, the have-nots of modern history, ought not be sacrificed or traded as political pawns when Uncle Sam sits at the table garbed in the stars and stripes of liberty and justice. The United States, as champion of the weak, the deprived, the defrauded, could conceivably bring a salutory new alignment in world politics and strike a blow for peace in some of the areas where eruptions are sure to come unless justice is speedily accomplished.

Nearer home, the voice of Washington diplomacy, being a respecter of the *status quo,* cannot cite the real issues increasing in tempo and intensity among our Latin American neighbors. Can and should Christians speak to the heart of the problem? Long impoverished republics, whose people have been enslaved by politician and prelate, are ripe for the advance of Communism. Fanned dry of spiritual values, stripped of land and liberty by inept rulers and an entrenched church, South and Central America are not merely potential danger zones. They are tinderboxes, inflammable in the extreme, certain centers of conflagration on our very borders. The least skilled analyst or political observers can foresee the entry of subversive, then overt, Communism into territories perfectly tailored for its false promises to desperate people. Future wars are in the plotting state now.

It may not be too late to raise the clamor for justice in pan-America. It would lose us friends in Rome. It might gain us our souls—and our lives.

Will history ever suggest of evangelical churches of the twentieth century that we were worthy to raise issues? How else can we do anything except cry mockingly, "Peace, peace," when there is no peace?

The Call to Effective Propaganda

There is no defense for the naiveté displayed by American diplomacy in the realm of propaganda. There can be no pardon for our own officials whose arrogance and greed have misappropriated funds allocated for foreign aid and relief. Nor is it understandable, apart from incredible gullibility, how so many authenticated instances have appeared of misuses of aid sent by American generosity to alleviate human needs. When goods and tools and clothing and cash fall into the greedy hands of overlords or underlings, or when American goods are distributed with Communist labels on the packages, then these are moral issues and Christian protests are in order. We are not that helpless in rendering our merciful ministries, and the force of this tremendous factor for peace and good will is blunted when we do not use such a legitimate project for peaceful ends. Blessed might we be if we learn to "toot our own horn" where it could be profitably heard.

The Christian has other concerns at the point of propagandizing—for this is his stock in trade. He has good news to be told, a story to get through to men to win them. He knows that the character of the message partakes of the character of the messenger. Therefore the quality of the men who represent the government and the people of the United States is of considerable point to him. Admittedly it is impossible to make thoroughgoing Christian character a requirement for the State Department and all diplomatic or consular service, but church members ought not to be mute at the issue of men of principle and character in our foreign service. While the spectre of "the ugly American" does not hang over every embassy, the sons of peace shudder at the image many diplomats reflect of life in this land of Christian birth.

Christian interest is also aroused by the potential for peace in the lives of the American servicemen who are on duty in vast areas of the earth. They are avenues of peace—or conflict. And they come from homes and churches which thus have an open line to millions the world over. I have heard from a reliable reporter of the G. I.s in Japan who in drunken celebration of New Year's Eve pursued and struggled with some Japanese girls who had just left a Baptist school to go home after watch night services. The girls broke away and ran back to the refuge of the college. There was a prominent Japanese man who had almost been won by the American missionary. After this incident, he announced flatly to the missionary that he was never to speak to him again about Christ. He left the church in bitterness and never returned. On the other hand, the largest Baptist church in Japan was organized by G. I.s who attended the then nondenominational church and faithfully sat and read their Testaments while the Japanese pastor preached in a tongue they did not know. He was so impressed that he asked Dr. Edwin Dozier what these Baptist boys believed. When told, he responded, "We believe that, too; can we be Baptists?" They could, and are!

There remain at least some avenues of communication through government and government service open to those who are concerned with the things that make for peace. The American story, as well as the Christian story, must be told persuasively and well.

The Summons to Christian Aggression

The blessedness assured to peacemakers offers no consolation to those who are merely peace lovers. These, indeed, may allow a threatening situation to worsen because they deplore disturbance, and thereby increase the likelihood of tragic consequences. Peace has to be "waged."

Christian love is aggressive, is intrusive. A twelve-year-old boy returned from Sunday morning services and related to his parents how his Sunday School teacher had talked with him that day about becoming a Christian. The mother remarked tartly, "It looks as though he could have attended to his own business!" The lad answered soberly, "Mother, if you could have been there and heard him as he talked to me, you would have felt that it *was* his business."

The gospel intrudes. Its salt, its leaven, its light were not meant to be self-contained. They move out in widening circles, wanted or not. Invitations are not prerequisites.

Sometimes the strategy is deliberate compassion and good will, both hard to resist. Love is the golden key to the human heart and gains entry more often than not. The small boy put it in irreducible terms. "Ronnie treated me mean when we were playing ball. He made me mad. I went home and got my new baseball bat. I came back and found Ronnie. I let him use my new bat. Me and Ronnie's friends." It is the world's oldest peace plan.

Good will is something more than the pious and doubtful hope that the dog will not bite. It is a positive confidence and affection that transmits itself to the beast and soothes his aggressions. If you can do that *you* are the aggressor and the victor. Love people and they will know it, and the less they expect the warm acceptance of themselves the more effect it will have upon them when that acceptance is manifested. Once a man flung a pail of water on Archaelaus, the Macedonian. The enemy expected to be attacked, at least berated. Archaelaus said nothing at all; the other, thoroughly frustrated, moved away and puzzled over the turn of affairs. When a friend asked the Macedonian how he could bear the insult so serenely, he said, "He threw the water not on me, but on the man he thought I was." Men of ill will cannot handle men of good will.

It is the principle of spiritual jujitsu. Bend the way the enemy does not expect. Take him off guard. Jesus called it *striking* with the other cheek, *capturing* a man in the trap of a second mile. This is real Christian aggression. It is the heart of the Gospel, and if it is not practical, does not work, then we have no Gospel. God wagered all on the efficacy of love to change men, to win men, to make peace. For love is not something you observe. It is not a thin picture on a flat screen. It has the third dimension of depth. Like a zoom lens on a camera, it reaches out and focuses on *you*. You are involved. If you are loved, you love. Love begets love. We love "because he first loved us" (I John 4:19). Love is living goodwill, the merging of the ego into others in order to impart one's self to another without losing that self.

Dr. M. T. Rankin, missionary statesman, spoke prophetically when he used to depict how American ships sailed into far eastern ports and dropped anchor at dockside. On the passenger decks hundreds of eager tourist faces looked into the thousands of impassive faces of people who lived there. There was a term for them. They were "natives." The very word had a patronizing ring, the ugly implication that they were still "foreigners" even when they stood on their own soil. In expansive glee some would toss money into the bay and half nude boys would dive for the prize of a "useless" coin equal to their day's wage. An elderly grandmother, in obvious poverty, raised a sack on a long bamboo pole in hopes of getting a larger gift. In strange detachment a passenger obliged. The loudspeaker summoned all those who had signed up for the tour of the "native quarter," and they went and jostled by the throngs, saw the filth, smelled the smells, bargained for silks, returned to the ship, bathed and dressed and sat down to rich food on snowy cloths and sailed out into the clean ocean, and left the people deeply infuriated. Then came 1941, and the Japanese could do more than hate, they could kill. In steaming jungle and on volcanic islands the white man reaped the bad harvest of his intolerable pride.

The Chinese still looks for his day of reckoning!

What if we had given ourselves to them? What if love had warmly accepted, identified with, other men as they were? What, indeed, if Christians now had enough aggression of love to disclose themselves and give themselves? It is eternally written, "Whoever would save his life will lose it, and whoever loses his life for my sake will find it" (Matthew 16:25 RSV).

Such is God's revelation. He did not survey our moral filth and rags from celestial heights and grasp the prize to remain apart. He set no cross in a public place with neon signs attached to each arm and an amplifier intoning, "God loves you." He came to us, he identified with us even in our sin; he died with a loving Father's look. Who can deny His revelation of love?

Like God—like people? God grant that it may be so!

The Force of a Dramatic Example

What impetus could be given to the Christian's, and America's, bid for peace in the earth if opportunity were found to dramatize our peaceful desire! When the United States used the indemnity levied against China as a result of the Boxer Rebellion to grant scholarships to Chinese young people in American universities, a thrill of goodwill went throughout the world. This was truly *making* peace!

In more recent times the hospital ship "Hope" stood white, clean, and inviting in Far and Middle East harbors—a living example of mercy and love, and in a form not corruptible by other governments or officials.

How good it would be if disaster relief could sometimes be given by plain American citizens, including young people, rather than by soldiers in uniform. Even if some requirement of training were enforced, such as perhaps by a Red Cross disaster squad, the sight and experience of average citizens serving with their own hands and giving from their own love of giving would inevitably leave its impression on a grateful people.

There is drama in men's souls, and the message of peace ought to be embodied and performed, not merely declared.

Admittedly it is a fantasy (were not most realities once fantasies?), but what might be accomplished by an "Operation Open Door"? It is perhaps conceded that exchange programs (student exchange, teacher exchange, or cultural exchange) represent the best avenues of that understanding which makes for peace. Could we dare propose a program so vast that masses of persons at all levels of society would literally invade the lives of men in all the countries of the world?

What if each of the member states of the United Nations was invited to prepare its three largest or three most typical cities for a mass exchange with three American cities of somewhat comparable size? Three hundred communities in this nation would prepare to receive large delegations from the companion cities and send their own overseas to them. Most of the countries of the world would be affected. This country might experience its greatest moral and spiritual awakening. The mayors and councils would exchange functions for a period of time. Other civic officials, law enforcement officers, leaders in education, science, and the humanities, artists and composers and authors, legislators, judges, religious leaders, librarians, doctors, labor leaders and laborers, manufacturers, musicians, festival boards, and public commissioners—all these would spend the stipulated time being involved in the counterpart activities of those at home. Three hundred American neighborhoods would get to know and care about faraway places in a hundred nations. And three hundred delegations would return to their homelands less susceptible to propaganda about this "capitalistic, warmongering republic," which actually bears little resemblance to the image held by the masses of the world.

The cost would be exceeded only by the planning involved—

both astronomical. But that cost (only a few days of present military billions) could be borne by the United States, and as a good investment in peace. It may be dismissed as very unreal, utterly implausible. It would require support from the President of the United States down to the boards of deacons in the local churches. Yet the force of such an Operation Open Door to the world might give its name to a new era.

Let someone in government and someone in religion come up with a better plan. But let the drama of peaceful men be played by the men, not their statesmen. To play the role might be to learn it!

The Courage for a New Departure

In a final effort to achieve practicality on a most impractical subject, there are some adventures for today's churches that might be warranted. It is patently difficult to make new departures when some of the old methods are tried and true; and there is never a guarantee that the new ones will work.

There is, for instance, no effective "day" for the expressions and promotion of world peace. Granted the method is a bit shopworn, but one wonders if this nation does not benefit immeasurably in the grace of gratitude because of the traditional Thanksgiving Day observance. Would a World Day of Peace offer any leaven?

There is some history at this point. During the Crusades came the Truce of God, advocated by synods and Councils of the Roman Church, which attempted to suspend hostilities on certain days and at specified seasons. Even in a world of conquest, the armies on both sides ceased operations from Thursday to Sunday inclusive, from Advent to eight days after Epiphany, and during Easter. This is a poor and shallow answer to war, but one also remembers that at Christmastime soldiers in the trenches of the Civil War and World War I observed an unofficial truce while men heard the sounds of Christmas carols rather than the whine of the sniper's bullet. Such occasional truces in Vietnam have also provided glimpses of hope on that tragic scene.

Christians really do not know what to do with Christmas.

Could this be the answer? Give up the tinsel and the commercial orgy and turn the observance into a pageant of peace. There is good scriptural authority in the declaration of the angels at the initial announcement. Let the gifts be to other peoples in other nations; the Christmas offerings for missions are already a beginning. Let the theme turn to practical steps for peace. New carols could be born, new drama material discovered, new appeals made to other nations to adopt December 25 as a day for a pageant of world peace, new Sunday School lessons prepared, new sermons preached. It might make the old, old story very new indeed.

On another front, there is a daring hope that new techniques and procedures might supplement our Christian world mission enterprises. The future of Christian missions may wait on the world of the lay missionary, not as a substitute but as an extension of the full-time appointee.

"Operation Brother's Keeper" demonstrated the validity of this approach when a team of physicians went around the world at their own expense, ministered to millions in Christian compassion, then returned to their practices and rendered a splendid account of their mission's stewardship all over America.

The time has come when a vastly expanded Christian missionary "Peace Corps" should be made operative. Technical people could give a year; some over sixty might give a lifetime; students would give two years; teachers, a sabbatical year; doctors, six months. Transportation and open doors offer new circumstances. The speed of world madness offers new motive. The need of an impression in force offers eloquent reason to consider a new departure.

Father Divine used to say that we metaphysicians always find it difficult to tangibilitate. These suggestions, however, have been offered as tentative but hopeful steps, not matured or even tested plans for peace.

We need a place to begin; perhaps this is it. Christians have a Lord to command. So, "Arise, and let us be going," for "Blessed are the peacemakers."

11.

PRACTICAL STEPS FOR PEACE

CHARLES WELLBORN
Chaplain
Florida State University
Tallahassee, Florida

"The dogmas of the quiet past are inadequate to the stormy present: the occasion is piled high with difficulty, and we must think anew and act anew."

Remarkably modern in tone and sentiment, these words might have been written yesterday. Actually, they appear in the Annual Message to Congress, delivered by Abraham Lincoln on December 1, 1862. That they were spoken a hundred years ago makes them no less relevant to our circumstance today. Consider our situation.

Though we pride ourselves on our advances in every field of science and culture, we are living in what Dr. Pitirim Sorokin has demonstrated is, literally, the bloodiest century in all recorded history.

Though we have dramatically invaded space and are probing toward the moon, we seem powerless to deal with the tensions and passions that array nation against nation in destructive violence.

Though we pour millions of dollars and long hours of research into the quest for controls and cures for terrible diseases like cancer and polio, we, at the same time, invest billions of dollars and a major section of our scientific genius in the never-ending search for more effective instruments of war and destruction.

Certainly, President Lincoln's words could apply to us. Poorly equipped with outworn concepts and patterns of thought and action we are facing a new age. We have adjusted technologically to the nuclear era, but, psychologically, emotionally, and spiritually, most of us, even those of us who are Christians, are still living in the gasoline age, if not the horse-and-buggy days.

By this, it is not implied that the central and historic affirmations of our Christian faith are outmoded and old-fashioned. The Gospel never goes out of style. But the task of each generation of Christian disciples is the application of these affirmations to the pressing problems of contemporary life. New wine bursts old wine sacks, and the heady and disturbing new wine of the nuclear age has long since burst the mental and spiritual containers which we found adequate for another era. Unhappily, too many of us refuse to recognize that the wine sacks are leaking. We go superficially on our way, blissfully unaware that when the time of testing comes, as it may at any moment, we shall find the wine sack empty.

What does the nuclear age demand of the followers of Jesus of Nazareth? If, under the dominion of God's Spirit, Christians today are, in Lincoln's words, "to think and act anew," what will this involve? What does the Lord require of us?

Our prime concern here is with the problem of peace, not because it is the only problem, but because its dimensions intersect virtually every other crisis of our time. Peace may mean, of course, purely an inner state which produces courage, security, and assurance in a time of personal strain and crisis. "Peace I leave with you; my peace I give unto you," the Master promised. Certainly the appropriation of this peace by redeemed men and women is a prime concern of the Gospel. The realization of such inner spiritual peace is an intensely individual matter, and there can be no substitute for person-to-person Christian witness and the sharing of the Gospel truth. This kind of peace comes neither automatically nor independently. Peace within a human life is the product of an even more basic kind of peace—that between man and God. The Gospel is a message of reconciliation, proclaiming the good news that the death and resurrection of Jesus Christ has battered down the wall of separation between a holy God and sinful men. Man may be united by faith with his Creator. The alienation of sin may be replaced by the peace of reconciliation. To proclaim this message is the prime obligation of the church of Jesus Christ. No more practical step toward the objective can be listed.

Basic, primary, and essential as this kind of peace is to the Christian, are we entitled to stop here? Is the Christian life purely an introspective and individual matter, involving only peace between man and God? The New Testament will not sustain such an interpretation. Its clear teaching is that men who are at peace with God are constrained to seek peace with their fellow man. Reconciliation with God is the source of reconciliation with man. What is the Great Commandment? Jesus said, "Thou shalt love the Lord thy God with all thy heart, and with all thy soul, and with all thy mind." Then He turned that commandment over like a coin and read the reverse and inseparable side, ". . . Thou shalt love thy neighbor as thyself" (Matt. 22:36-40).

A right relationship between God and man is one of reconciliation and peace. A right relationship between man and man is one of peace and reconciliation. Nations are political entities which consist of groups of men, and the right relationship between nations, by God's standard, is also one of peace and reconciliation.

All of this may sound trite, but it is fundamentally important. Unhappily, many Christians in our time, under the pressures of the moment, want to identify a relationship among nations other than one of peace as the will of God. Some of them want to consecrate the cold war and convert it into a holy crusade. They see themselves as instruments of God's judgment, deceiving themselves into believing that all the righteousness, justice, and goodness lies on only one side of the barriers which divide our world, while all the sin and evil is on the other side. They are the spiritual sons of the Pharisees, pronouncing God's judgments for Him and ready to forget that they themselves, like all other men, stand under these same judgments and are revealed as sinners by them.

The truth which must be faced is that no relationship less than peace and reconciliation among men and nations can be accepted as the ultimate will of the God of our Lord Jesus Christ. The cold war, as all wars, is not God's will; it is a product of sin—the sin of the Communist in his atheistic materialism and lust for world dominion—but also the sin of men like you and me, who have failed as individuals and as a nation to live out the perfect will of a God of love, holiness, and peace.

If we are to speak in terms of practical steps toward peace among nations perhaps the place to begin is with the puncturing of the fragile but dangerous balloon of our own self-righteousness. The prophets of old—Jeremiah, Hosea, Amos, Isaiah and the rest—found it necessary to remind Israel again and again that she had no unshakeable monopoly on the favor of God. The long road of civilized history is lined with the bleached bones of cultures, kingdoms, and national powers who trusted in their own strength and exaggerated their own moral perfection. All of us know that one of the easiest and most popular pastimes of our day is to confess the sins of the Communists. We assiduously devote our energies to pointing out every defect and danger, every evil and inconsistency in the Communist stance. Well and good! But what of our own position? Is there thorough integrity and consistent moral fiber in the cloth of our own culture? What of the hatred, the injustice, the prejudice, the oppression, the crime, the lust which are undeniable parts of our own national pattern? Which is most urgent for us in God's eyes? Is it for us to confess the sins of the Russians and the Chinese, or to confess our own?

This is no attempt to equate the Russian and American ways of life, or to say that one is just as bad as the other, and that it therefore makes no real difference which one wins the present world struggle. There is a necessity for Americans to reaffirm their faith in the basic truth of their own convictions about freedom and justice, but let us not forget that the very ability to manifest some signs of national humility is one of the significant marks of the infinite superiority of the free way of life over that of the Communists.

I remember a conversation with a young Italian at the Brussels World's Fair in 1958. We had met casually while visiting the American Exhibition Building on the fair grounds. A somewhat controversial part of the United States Exhibit was a section devoted to a consideration of some of our own unsolved problems—things like slum clearance, racial discrimination, and soil erosion. As we emerged from that part, my Italian friend shook his head in wonder. "It takes a great and powerful people to admit their own problems so frankly," he commented. "It is significant that the Russian building contains no such section."

We shall have taken one giant step toward peace if we are able, as a nation, honestly to recognize our own internal problems and wholeheartedly to give ourselves to the continuing task of finding solutions for these problems. We are a free people, but not a perfect people. We have no monopoly on righteousness, as our enemies have no monopoly on sin. The basis for even a minimum measure of international reconciliation among nations, as among men, is the recognition of a common predicament and a common need. Even if our enemies, dominated as they are by a materialistic philosophy of life, cannot or will not recognize and repent of their own sins, this is no excuse for our failure to recognize and repent of ours.

A second practical step toward peace is suggested. In the sense in which we are using the term, peace—that is, a relative peace among nations which enables the world to seek creative and constructive solutions to its difficulties and problems—can never be absolute. There is no possibility of eliminating every source of friction and disagreement, every conflict of interest and power. What we can seek is legitimate and non-destructive avenues by which these disagreements may be minimized and the conflicts adjusted. A world without force, violence, or sin is not a real possibility, from the Christian viewpoint. But a world without armed and irresponsible warfare among nations is a live option, though a difficult one.

What practical step will contribute to that kind of world? One thing that will help significantly is a healthy dose of the truth. Of course, it is hard to know what the truth is. It very often is uncomfortable. This makes even more imperative the struggle to find it. If the truth were handed out free on the street corners, this might be a different world. But it costs effort and dedication to know the truth in these days. The issues of war and peace in an atomic age are exceedingly complex and highly technical. We need all the patience, common sense, and calm reasoning we can muster for the facing of these problems. To borrow another's phrase, our problems are too delicate, the consequences too ominous, for us to tackle them with our glands instead of our brains.

Understand that thoughtful men need not be the foes of honest emotion. We are inevitably, if we have any deep convictions at all, emotionally involved in the problems of freedom, war, and peace. But emotion is healthy only when it is founded on fact, not fiction.

Recently, I attended a public meeting at which a man in a place of responsible leadership passionately addressed the group, pleading with them in the name of patriotism and Americanism to support a move to withdraw the United States from the United Nations. This is, of course, a legitimate position for an American citizen to hold. I did not object to the man's right to believe as he did nor to his passion. What did upset me was his distortion of truth. For the most part, he made vague appeals without substantiation or documentation. When he did present what he represented as authoritative, my personal study and observation compelled me to conclude that about half of his so-called facts were falsehoods, while many of the remaining allegations, although approximately true, were ripped out of context, incomplete, and misinterpreted.

What a great step toward peace might be taken if men would

refuse to accept everything they hear at face value. We need to question seriously the veracity of the man who is obviously grinding a personal political ax. We are justified in considerable skepticism about those who tell us that they have all the truth, while they insist that the great bulk of the nation's leadership is either subversive or deluded. We rightly refuse to place any confidence in the Communist propagandist, for we know that he is committed to the proposition that the end justifies the means. Therefore, he may use any means or method; but the same caution must apply to those in our own country who, while embracing high and noble purposes and ends, at the same time, in grudging or perhaps unrealized admiration of Communist success in the world, adopt the Communist methods. The end does not justify the means, either for the Communist or for the freedom-loving American. We do not fight error with falsehood, lack of integrity with intellectual dishonesty, slander with vicious name-calling, group prejudice with guilt-by-association. Our Christian faith can tell us that. Rather, the kind of method we use inevitably shapes and forms the structure of our purposes. If our methods are wrong, our goals will also suffer.

In contrast, we can safely put more weight on the testimony of those who, without much possibility of personal or political gain, seek objectively to study and amass facts without regard for how these facts affect particular partisan positions. The people who are not running for anything and who are more interested in truth than in the manipulation of it are, generally speaking, the most reliable sources of information. This is important, for much conflict, even on an international scale, arises from reliance on fiction rather than fact, propaganda rather than reason, fear and prejudice rather than sanity and confidence.

Humility and honesty may not sound like great factors in the struggles of the nation, but these are areas in which individual citizens have great opportunity to make their personal influence felt.

A third practical step toward peace to which I would call attention involves the exercise of yet another homely virtue—that of patience. Patience is usually neither popular nor glamorous; to advocate its employment is to expose oneself to attack as a defeatist, a coward, or a compromiser. But the struggle for peace is neither simple nor easy, and if, as we Americans must insist, peace is to be joined with freedom, then the task becomes doubly difficult. Some people are actually more afraid of peace than they are of war. Writing in the *U. S. Naval Institute Proceedings,* Lt. Commander John F. Riley expresses the situation in this way, ". . . The era of peace is far more dangerous to our ultimate survival than a time of war. In war the problem is simple—survive and win. In peace, however, world and home politics exert tremendous pressures. The problems become complex indeed, beset with imponderables and lashed by the spirit of nationalism and the battle of ideologies."

Simply put, the cold war is not the right kind of weather for most Americans. We are accustomed to tackling a job and seeing it through to successful conclusion as rapidly as possible. The present world stalemate leaves us frustrated and bellicose. While the Russian, speaking broadly, is a political animal *par excellence,* weaned on dialectics and conspiracy, the average American equates politics with pork barrel and baby-kissing and wants as little to do with it as possible. The devious, rough-and-tumble, rabbit-punching, advancing, retreating, thrusting maneuvers in the contemporary international arena are not for us. Impatient with the careful sparring of diplomacy, we are eager to hear the words of those who propose dramatic, overnight solutions and promise glorious and complete victory at once over the enemies of freedom. Thus, a nationally syndicated columnist puts it this way: "My own convictions are that peace is a 'myth' word, that we are universally at war with Communism, that our generation or the next will have to shoot it out, and that there is a very good argument for do-it-now."

The man in the street may not say it so eloquently, but he longs for some master key to conflict; he wants to "get it over with," "to do it now." But clear thinking must remind us that it is a horribly empty victory which presides over the scattered debris of three or more continents and 250 megacorpses. Sanity requires that we recognize that World War II took our nation, even in victory, a giant step toward internal totalitarianism and that a thermonuclear conflict would almost certainly produce a military police state in what was left of this land of freedom and justice. Which is more important, the phantasm of quick and easy victory, at the possible risk of the destruction of both civilization and freedom, or the long, hard, painful, frustrating struggle toward a world of peace, order, law, and justice? This question the individual Christian citizen must help to answer.

Practical steps for peace must include humility, honesty, patience, and one other basic virtue: confidence. Indeed, this virtue is double-barrelled. The cause of world peace desperately needs men and women possessing confidence in their own values and way of life, and also possessing holy confidence, faith in God.

Why is it that in times of national crises, so many Americans press the panic button? Is it because they lack confidence in the strength of the very system of government and way of life they profess to love? Our nation is founded on the fundamental of freedom; yet, the inevitable response of some people to any threat to freedom is, ironically, to curtail and limit that freedom. Many of our spiritual forefathers were in various minority groups, professing unpopular and subversive ideas, writing and publishing "dangerous" literature, and delivering inflammatory speeches. Society and its power structures reacted as they almost always do, not with more freedom but with less. Our spiritual forebears were arrested, dispossessed of home and property, jailed, gagged, hunted, tortured, and killed. Did all this silence their ideas or suppress their so-called heresy? Obviously not. Why is it that so many learn from history, but so often the wrong lessons? Look at that history: Nero and his persecution of the Christians, the Anabaptist suffering of the sixteenth century, the terrors of the Spanish Inquisition, the persecution of nonconformists in colonial America. What does history teach? It teaches that the surest way to spread an idea is to burn the book that contains it, that the quickest way to broadcast a philosophy is to hang the man who devised it. There is no answer to tyranny except freedom, and more freedom. It must be responsible freedom; it must be freedom under God. But, make no mistake, it must be real freedom, not tyranny garbed in the garments of hypocrisy.

If we believe in the essential rightness of the democratic concept of the worth of every human personality under God, if we honestly believe that "all men are created equal and are endowed by their Creator with certain inalienable rights," then, as Christian citizens, let us trust our system confidently in the crucible of life and history. We need not fight Communism with Communist machinations, nor need we fear the eventual outcome of any honest confrontation of Marxist tyranny with freedom and justice. This is why we can be patient, because we know that, though we ourselves are sinful men, we have, by the grace of God, discovered values of life and personality that are eternally enduring.

But the Christian can couple this confidence in the values of freedom and justice with a greater and deeper faith which rests on the sovereignty of God and the Lordship of Jesus Christ. Without such faith, with what are men left in this age of terror? Obviously, if we are to believe the wild-eyed spokesmen of disaster, there is no hope left except the desperate gamble of nuclear war. The atomic strategists talk about using nuclear power in a "rational" and measured fashion. What this means, as one of them has explained, is that a non-nuclear provocation by the Soviets might be met by a limited American thermonuclear reprimand. Suppose the Russians take over West Berlin; we retaliate by bombing Kiev and Leningrad. The Russians respond by wiping Pittsburgh and Atlanta off the map. Then we meet with the Russians somewhere and talk the whole thing over. This, some imply, is the civilized and rational way to go about things.

But the Christian is not limited to this kind of bleak prospect. In the providence of the God of love and peace, there must be other alternatives, options which preserve both relative peace and increasing freedom. In faith, the Christian citizen must support his government in a continuing search for these alternatives, refusing to give ear to these fatalists who tell us there is no avoiding a final nuclear showdown.

Christians need not be afraid of negotiation. Negotiation is not synonymous with appeasement, if we negotiate from strength —both the strength of national power and that of moral principle. Talking with our enemies is not equivalent to surrender, and every international conference is not an automatic sellout. As Christian citizens, committed irrevocably by our Gospel to the cause of peace, we must throw our weight behind honest, hard-headed, realistic attempts to find a path of peace through the perilous mine field of modern international relationships.

Dr. Henry Kissinger, perhaps America's outstanding authority in the area of atomic military strategy, has declared that in the present state of technology an arms race is an extremely unstable form of security. Observing that the next few years may afford us our last opportunity to stabilize the arms race by means of negotiation, he acknowledges the possibility that Communist obdurancy may doom our most earnest efforts. He says it would be unforgivable, however, if we failed because of our refusal to face either the importance or the complexity of the challenge.

In faith and confidence, Christians should be in the forefront of a popular demand that we face that challenge squarely, unflinchingly, and intelligently.

This study of peace is now brought to a close with some brief, obvious, but hopefully significant suggestions for concrete action on the part of Christian citizens in the struggle for peace:

(1) Make yourself a truth-and-information committee of one. The amount of falsehood, trash, and immoral propaganda that is being poured into the American mind by the apostles of hate, discord, slander, and war is almost unbelievable. But there is truth available. I could wish that every Christian woman might find time to become involved with the League of Women Voters and its program of factual information. I could wish that Christian men might get the habit of challenging the sources and the motives of those who preach hate, sow distrust, and defame

character. I could wish that all of us together could rise up against every attempt to throttle truth, harness freedom, destroy liberty, or subvert the basic rights of any man, black or white, rich or poor, Catholic, Jew, or Protestant, educated or unlearned, every little human being anywhere.

(2) Involve yourself on the side of decency, human dignity, truth, and peace in the political struggles of your community, state, and nation. True, there is no perfect political party, no Christian party platform. There are no perfect candidates for office. But, thank God, in most of this country, we have a choice, and in each situation there will be grounds for a reasonable decision. One man is a better man for the office than another, and in each situation, one party will be more trustworthy than the other. But the making of such choices and the personal involvement which ought to follow such a choice cannot be done lightly. We must delve deeply into the issues. Whether a candidate smokes or drinks is not the final measure of his qualification. The crisis of our day demands leadership by men with deep convictions about such fundamentals as truth, human dignity, equal justice, and the responsible search for peace.

(3) It may sound trite and pious, but many of us pay lip service to, but neglect in practice, the ministry of prayer. Pray for peace, peace with justice, peace with order, peace with freedom. And pray for those who carry the almost unbearable load of responsibility in our nation. It does not really matter what you think personally about the nation's President. Whatever we may think of him, he is our President, by the vote of the nation. And we know that, regardless of the jokes about him, he stands today on the loneliest spot on earth. His responsibilities are awesome and frightening; the peace of the whole world depends, in part, upon his actions. Pray for him and for those who labor with him.

Humility, honesty, patience, confidence, faith, service, prayer—are these really practical? They are, after all, the fundamental virtues of the Christian faith. In their practice lies the Christian contribution to the struggle for peace.